MOMENTS ON THE MOREAU

TULSA

ISBN: 978-1-957262-90-1
Moments on the Moreau
Copyright © 2023 by Jeremy Paul Ämick
Yorkshire Publishing
1425 E 41st Pl
Tulsa, OK 74105
www.YorkshirePublishing.com
918.394.2665
Published in the USA

MOMENTS ON THE
MOREAU

A Historical Journey Through Mid-Missouri

JEREMY PAUL ÄMICK

Contents

Acknowledgments

T here are countless individuals who have kindled my interest in history and are in some way responsible for creations such as this book. Gert Strobel, though you have passed on, I remain ever grateful for the hours you invested throughout your life to preserve stories from Lohman and the surrounding areas. Roger Buchta, you have also left us, but let me express my appreciation for the many times you have shared with me your passion for our local history. Additionally, Don Buchta, you have selflessly discussed with me so much of your local historical research and I am proud to count you among my friends. Many others in our local communities, such as my mother, Linda Amick, and my competent editor, Dennis Hall, have also contributed in some fashion. Others scattered throughout the Moreau River region have been of great inspiration and assistance, and though your names may not be printed here, please know that your unwavering passion for historical preservation is recognized and appreciated.

Dedication

To the pioneering souls who strived to build our Mid-Missouri communities. I pray that we remain good stewards of all which you have left us and that the sacrifices you have made for future generations are never forgotten.

Moments on the Moreau
A Historical Journey Through Mid-Missouri

The Moreau River is a well-known and central feature of Mid-Missouri. This smaller river and its tributaries pass through many communities in this region and have a collateral influence on others. Its primary and secondary waters flow under highways, irrigate farms, pass by homes perched on bluffs and, in other locations, drift through smaller settlements. It is a waterway possessing a legacy that spans several counties and has either directly or indirectly touched an assortment of communities in some fashion. These communities include such towns as Russellville, Lohman, Enon, Honey Creek, Jefferson City, Brazito, Hickory Hill, and California. It should be of little surprise, then, that a compilation of historical stories from around Mid-Missouri would have a title somehow connected to the Moreau River.

In the vicinity of its waters have emerged many interesting stories throughout the years including one from a former slave who lived to the impressive age of 113 years old. This story is followed by an area Lutheran congregation that had the privilege of hearing from a Native American Christian missionary who became the last chief of the Mohican tribe. Some of these happenings feature stories that could serve as the basis for blockbuster Hollywood films, such as a young man hailing from the community of Hickory Hill who became a lawman in a bustling Wild West town. However, he later engaged in unsavory behaviors and all but disappeared from family history after moving to Guatemala.

This is a collection of stories that highlights people like James Valentine Ambrose—a man who participated in the California gold rush and eventually settled near Brazito. It was in his later years that his name was gifted to a community and a one-room schoolhouse in the area. And just as education was important to the Ambrose family, one-room schoolhouses became a common site in many communities throughout Mid-Missouri, representing the primary point of education for area youth. Some of these worn buildings now serve new purposes for their current owners while others have been torn down and relegated to the memories and recollections of the aged population who attended classes within them. These schools, however, do not simply represent the buildings that held students, but the many teachers who dedicated years of their lives to providing a stellar education, thus recognizing their reward was not in the meager salaries they received but the future successes of those they instructed.

Several stories emerging near the banks of the Moreau and its tributaries are connected to the many businesses that have contributed to the daily lives of local residents. A car dealership that began in Jamestown and later moved to Tipton, and eventually into the town of California, would go on to achieve the century mark—a rare distinction in the automotive industry. Or perhaps it might include a young man raised in one of the oldest families in the Lohman area, who went on to establish himself as a respected building contractor in the county. The once bustling community of Brazito also served as home to many thriving business ventures such as a garage that now serves as a convenience store. The community of Centertown, which was once situated along the main artery known as U.S. Highway 50, became home to a popular dance hall known as Dixie Gardens. Prior to burning to the ground in 1947, this location thrived as a major entertainment venue and even hosted shows by famed comedian Sid Caesar.

The stories of these communities and those who built them cannot be adequately described without also connecting them to the history of houses of worship. When settlements grew throughout Mid-Missouri and along the Moreau River, one of the priorities for the pioneering families was to establish churches where they could worship with like-minded individuals. Fortunately, many of these churches have survived and continue to thrive, revealing a history to be shared thanks to farsighted individuals who sought to protect, preserve, and share that history.

For several years now, I have been writing and researching the fascinating stories couched within the communities of Mid-Missouri and am always impressed with the new ones I learn about daily, many of which beckon my attention and yearn to be uncovered. When you begin to pull on the thread of a local folk tale or historical event, you often discover that it is connected to many people and places . . . and, in the end, more stories come pouring forth—just like the waters of the Moreau. This compilation, I assure you, is in no way presented as a final package of events that have unfolded in Mid-Missouri in previous decades. Rather, it represents a snapshot of several of the people and places that have come before us.

It is my hope that these stories capture your interest and might in some way connect you to that which has come and, in many cases, passed on. Regardless, history continues to be made following the sunset of each day and I look forward to being able to share our fascinating local history, so long as the Good Lord grants me the opportunity. Enjoy this history from along the Moreau River, which is your history . . . our history.

Jeremy P. Ämick
Russellville, Missouri
May 2023

CHAPTER 1

The People

Eliza Sears – Centertown

Eliza Bruner was born to slaves in Linn Creek on February 14, 1832. When only two years old, she was separated from her family, sold for $200, and brought to live and work in the Centertown area. Her story became one of overcoming hardships, falling in love with a fellow slave, and later achieving the distinction of reaching the impressive age of 113 years old.

William Campbell Young, who brought Eliza Bruner to Cole County in 1834, was an Irish immigrant and pioneer resident of

Jefferson City. He served as the superintendent of construction for the building of the Missouri State Capitol that was completed in 1840. Historical records reveal that Young wore several hats that included being president and director of First National Bank in Jefferson City, building and operating mills near Centertown, elections as a county judge, in addition to receiving an appointment as a colonel in the state militia.

"The Judge's labors throughout life have been attended with good results, and he is now the owner of 900 acres of land (in the Centertown and Lohman areas)," shared a history of Cole County printed by Goodspeed's Publishing Company in 1889."

A funeral service was held at Centertown Baptist Church for Sears followed by her internment in Centertown Cemetery. Courtesy of Jeremy Amick

Yet of greater significance is the young Eliza Bruner, who fell in love with Joseph Williams, a fellow slave, while working on Young's expansive farm. The couple married in the late 1850s and welcomed two children in the coming years—Harvey and Joseph. Having been ripped from her family as a child, additional hardship was experienced by Eliza Williams after her husband enlisted in the 67th United States Colored Troops on January 14, 1865, three days after slavery was abolished in Missouri.

The *Daily Capital News* noted in the edition printed on March 2, 1945, that Eliza's husband "fought in the Union army in the Civil War . . . (and) . . . died before he reached home after receiving his discharge."

By the war's end, Eliza had received her freedom but now had two sons to raise alone. She remained self-sufficient and it is uncertain whether she received support from her former owner, W.C. Young. Despite his history as a slave owner, Young supported the education of African Americans, serving as a treasurer for the new Lincoln Institute (Lincoln University). As the years passed, someone invested the time and effort to teach Eliza how to read and write.

On May 31, 1868, she married her second husband, James Sears, with whom she had one son, William Robert. The brief ceremony was conducted by Andrew M. Elston, a county court judge who became the namesake for the Cole County community of Elston.

"James Sears was from the Mexico (Missouri) area," shared Lohman area resident Don Buchta, whose house sits on property once owned by W.C. Young. He added, "Apparently, her second husband did not want to work and she wasn't putting up with that, so she ran him off and he moved back to the Mexico area."

Buchta explained that the knowledge he has acquired regarding Eliza Sears predominantly came from Lohman natives Omar and Cletus Heidbreder, both of whom have since passed away.

"Back in the 1980s," Buchta said, "I went down to Eldon with one of the Heidbreders to interview an elderly gentleman about Eliza because he had known her."

Census records from 1900 reveal that Eliza was the head of household at her Centertown residence, living with two of her sons, a daughter-in-law, and a grandson.

"She lived in a small log cabin off a gravel road a short distance from Centertown," said Buchta. "It was explained to me that she worked for a local family babysitting and cooking. Also, I was told that there was a local man whose wife had died, leaving him with an infant, so she helped nurse the child."

Eliza leaned upon the reading and writing skills she had been taught, making lists of supplies she needed for both her own household and that of the family for whom she worked. She then took the list to Lohman to get the items.

"Even when she was up in her nineties, she would get on a horse and ride the five or six miles to the MFA in Lohman about every month," said Buchta. "She knocked on the door on the east side of the building, gave them her list, and then waited. They would bring out the flour, sugar, coffee . . . or whatever she had ordered, load it on her horse, and then she rode back home."

Growing older lost some of its grace since Eliza outlived two of her sons, one of whom was killed in a car accident in 1931 and another who died of heart failure in 1942. Two years later, age did bring with it one achievement that was highlighted in several newspapers.

"Oldest Missouri voter in the recent election was Mrs. Lizzie Sears, aged 112, who traveled three miles from her home southeast of Centertown . . . to the polls to cast her vote," reported the *Lincoln Clarion* on December 1, 1944. "Born in slavery, Mrs. Sears . . . has not missed voting in an election since the passing of the 19th amendment (ratified in 1920 and granting women the right to vote)."

The 113-year-old Eliza Sears died from pneumonia on February 25, 1945, and was laid to rest in Centertown Cemetery following services held at the local Baptist church.

Researching the former slave's story with great interest, Don Buchta remarked that although nothing more than a small grave marker denotes her lengthy life, he has found great satisfaction in learning of her legacy.

"I never met her, but she seemed like she was truly a remarkable person," he said. "She was a hard worker who came up in difficult times . . . and not too many people live to be 113." He added, "It's a fascinating story that needs to be shared." (*Photograph courtesy of Don Buchta.*)

Samuel W. Farmer – Hickory Hill

There are many fascinating characters emerging from the annals of Cole County history, some of whom possess stories lacking in virtuosity. Samuel W. Farmer, the son of a pioneering area family, demonstrated his effectiveness as a lawman in a Wild West town in Texas but went on to reveal a penchant for infidelity and a host of unsavory behaviors. Born in 1847 and raised on a farm near Eugene in southern Cole County, Samuel Farmer chose not to follow the agricultural influence of his father; instead, he pursued a career in law enforcement. In 1868, when only twenty-one years old, he became a constable within Clark Township and was for many years the town marshal for the once-bustling community of Hickory Hill.

The young lawman married his fiancée, Malinda J. Norfleet, in Cole County on June 11, 1872. His career in Missouri was soon curtailed when he developed medical complications that necessitated his move to more favorable climates during the winter of 1873.

"I have known [Samuel Farmer] from his boyhood," wrote Dr. William D. Jordan of Hickory Hill on March 10, 1879. "He was a constable of this township for many years. Made a good officer, gave general satisfaction as an officer." Dr. Jordan added, "[He] was attacked with hemorrhage of the lungs, and by my advice, as his physician, went to the state of Texas."

Information obtained from the Fort Worth Public Library notes that Farmer owned a stock farm in Wise County, Texas, and was accompanied in his move from Missouri by his childhood friends, J.C. Bond, J.P. Bass, and C.C. Simpson.

In the years after his arrival, the former Missourian made the move from Wise County to Tarrant County, settling in the rough and rowdy town of Fort

Raised on a farm near Eugene, Samuel Farmer gained law enforcement experience as the marshal for Hickory Hill. He was later elected town marshal in the Old West community of Ft. Worth, Texas. He is pictured with his second wife, Mattie.

Worth. In 1879, he was elected town marshal and was pictured wearing a custom-made badge along with a walrus-style mustache reminiscent of the famed western lawman Wyatt Earp.

"He was always fleet-footed from what I learned from my father," said Mike Taggart, a distant relative of Farmer. "He always enjoyed going on different ventures and ended up abandoning his first wife in Missouri, who later divorced him [in 1881]."

His ex-wife went on to marry Thomas W. Henley in 1882, with whom she raised several children. She passed away in 1916 and is interred in Spring Garden Cemetery in Miller County.

Remaining immersed in his law enforcement responsibilities, Farmer ran for reelection and on January 15, 1881, was described by the *Fort Worth Democrat* as ". . . an honest, brave, vigilant, unswerving, trustworthy and valuable officer to his people, and we have every reason to believe . . . that, if re-elected to this office, he will be the same in the future."

Family lore passed down through generation indicates Farmer spent his final years in Guatemala, where it is believed this photograph was taken. Courtesy of Mike Taggart

A history-laden moment in his career was linked to a gift from Sheriff Pat Garrett of Lincoln County, New Mexico. In December 1881, the *Fort Worth Democrat* explained, Garrett gave Farmer the cartridge belt and hat worn by famed outlaw Bill Bonney (Billy the Kid), when Garrett shot and killed him several months earlier.

While in Texas, Farmer met Mattie Johnson, and the two were married on July 28, 1883. Sadly, his record of abandonment would later compromise this relationship as well. The newspapers praised Farmer's performance as a law officer, citing him as a respected pillar of the community. But in 1893, his reputation suffered when he was sued for allegations of stealing a large sum of money from a suspect he had arrested for robbery.

He was later exonerated of the charges levied against him, but public opinion exposed its influence when he was not re-elected as city marshal of Ft. Worth. In 1895, he began the next step of his law enforcement career when appointed a Deputy U.S. Marshal and continued to make newspaper headlines.

The *Los Angeles Times* reported on February 28, 1895, ". . . Sam Farmer and his party had a fight with Ben Hughes and his gang of train robbers. Hughes was captured, and one of his men wounded." The paper added, "Snake Head, an Indian scout of Farmer's party, was killed."

Court records note that Farmer's wife discovered his history of infidelity. In proceedings filed in the District Court of Tarrant County in August 1896, she alleged: "during the months of August and September 1894 and a larger part of the years of 1893 and 1894, [Farmer] did clandestinely and stealthily consort with and have adulterous communications with one Pearl Clements and many other . . . prostitutes."

Additional allegations by his wife claimed that Farmer disappeared for long periods without providing notice of his whereabouts or any form of support, while also withdrawing from the bank large sums of money her parents had deposited in her personal account. Her request for divorce was granted. Family histories explain that Farmer was eventually sent to the country of Panama, where his duties as a Deputy U.S. Marshal became the apprehension of criminals with outstanding warrants in the United States.

"In later years, the family lost track of him but information was passed down through the family to my father [John R. Taggart], explaining that he eventually moved to Guatemala, where it is believed that he died and is buried," said Mike Taggart.

Taggart's father invested a fair amount of time researching the life of Samuel Farmer, never knowing for certain where or how he spent his final days. And though many details of the late lawman's life have morphed into mere speculation, he maintains that Farmer left a unique and interesting legacy.

"He certainly wasn't a paragon of virtue or someone whose personal life should be emulated, but he led a remarkable life full of uncommon experiences," Taggart said. *(Photographs courtesy of Mike Taggart.)*

James Valentine Ambrose – Ambrose Community

Many elements of the James Valentine Ambrose story cast the appearance of scintillating fiction, but are actually steeped in fact. Growing up in England in the early 1800s, he learned a trade from his father that helped sustain him after his immigration to the U.S. Years later, a school and community were named for him, but not before he made a small fortune in the gold rush, resulting in a legal embroilment that still serves as a cited example of case law.

"James Ambrose was my great-great-grandfather and was born in Liverpool, England on February 14, 1814, which is why he later added 'Valentine' as his middle name," shared Dr. Bill Ambrose. "His father was a carter and hired men to use horses and carts to transport goods from the docks in Liverpool, which was at the time the second busiest in the world."

While still in his teens and sometime after his father's death in 1830, James Ambrose came to Missouri, becoming one of the earliest settlers in an area near Brazito. Initially, he made a living using a horse and cart to transport coal from a mine in Brazito to the penitentiary in Jefferson City.

"We do not know a great detail about his first few years here but he returned to England in 1840 after his mother's death to settle his family's estate and receive whatever inheritance there might be," Dr. Ambrose explained.

Family records indicate that James Ambrose became a naturalized U.S. citizen in 1840 and the following year was married to Julia Ann Hoskins. Although he had been baptized in the Church of England, while living in Mid-Missouri he and his family became early members of the Primitive Baptist Church, his obituary explained.

In 1849, while living on a rented farm in the Brazito area, James Ambrose said goodbye to his wife and young son and headed to California during the gold rush with Alfred Bayse and N.S. Bachman. While traveling in Mexican territory and under the threat of abandonment by his partners, Ambrose signed a contract agreeing to several unreasonable stipulations.

"The other two did not stay in California for very long but my great-great-grandfather was out there for four years," said Dr. Ambrose. "I read a quote that noted he had a great avarice for gold and that his intention was to stay there until he had enough to live comfortably for the rest of his life . . . which he did," he added.

Upon returning to Missouri and reuniting with his family, Ambrose purchased an eighty-acre farm from Joseph Farmer. As the years passed, this farm grew to encompass 440 acres, stretching between Tanner Bridge Road and Route E. He and his wife became parents to six sons and five daughters; however, only one of his sons, Thomas, survived into adulthood. Ambrose and his wife later became members of a local Christian congregation but, despite his dedication to the scriptures, he clung to some of the vices he learned during his earlier trip to California.

"I found a record where he was arrested in Miller County for gambling but I am sure that was something he learned sitting around a campfire in the evenings while in a gold rush camp," Dr. Ambrose remarked.

His participation in the gold rush again showed its influence on his life when, in the mid-1850s, when he was sued by Alfred Basye for a breach of contract.

"Basye filed for damages of $1,000 in the Cole County court," Dr. Ambrose explained. "The judge was George Miller and he had to drop the case because his wife was Basye's sister." He continued, "The case was sent to Callaway County and they rendered a verdict on behalf of Ambrose. It was then appealed to the Missouri Supreme Court and Ambrose prevailed once again."

The majority opinion by the Missouri Supreme Court was authored by Judge William Scott, who also wrote the majority opinion in the famed Dred Scott case. *Basye v. Ambrose* is still utilized as case law with regard to liquidated damages and contract penalties.

As a farmer, James Ambrose raised crops on his expansive farm in an area off Tanner Bridge Road that became known as the Ambrose Community. An advocate of formal education, he erected a schoolhouse that was used by his children and their descendants, in addition to many students from the surrounding areas. The third iteration of this one-room schoolhouse still stands.

"He was a hardscrabble man even into his later years," Dr. Ambrose said. "The story is that he suffered from a spot of cancer on his face for many years and while he was at the barber in Old Bass [near Hickory Hill], he grabbed the razor and cut it off, but the cancer then spread."

The ninety-four-year-old passed away on April 20, 1908, and was described in his obituary as "one of the oldest settlers of the state and beyond a doubt, the oldest citizen of Cole County." He was laid to rest in the Hickory Hill Cemetery, where, eight years earlier, his beloved wife of sixty years had been buried.

Dr. Ambrose embraces opportunities to learn about his family's rich history and their contributions to the area, crediting his late Great Aunt Bessie "Bess" Pendleton for much of what has been preserved.

"Back in 1968, I would write my Great Aunt Bess, who was living in the Kansas City area, and ask her about her grandfather, James Ambrose," he said. "She shared with me much about his life, the Ambrose family and community, and even the Ambrose School." After a momentary pause for reflection, he concluded, "This has all been truly enjoyable to research, and had I not taken the time to communicate with Aunt Bess, so much of this history may have vanished." *(Photograph courtesy of Dr. Bill Ambrose.)*

John Perry "J.P." and Mary (Scheperle) Bass – Bass/Eugene

Cole County history was in its early years sprinkled with notations of the Bass family. In the southeastern section of the county, the Bass story began with a man who immigrated from an adjoining state and became a prominent farmer who had a small settlement named for him that is only remembered through the naming of a stretch of rural road. Metheldred Bass Sr. was born in Barren County, Kentucky in 1821, the same year Missouri achieved statehood. When still a young man, he settled in Cole County, where he married Perlina Apperson in 1843.

A worn newspaper article shared by his family on the Find A Grave website notes that Bass and his wife became parents to six children. His first wife was only forty-five years old when she died in 1871 and was laid to rest in the Hickory Hill Cemetery.

"Bass joined the Church of Christ near his home . . . and has been a devout and consistent member of the Mount Union congregation," the article explained.

Dedicated to making a living, Bass toiled in the field, raised livestock, and became a respected and well-known farmer in the southern section of Cole County. Soon, a small settlement began to unfold north of Eugene with the erection of a mercantile organized by several local farmers, which was later supplemented with a post office. Since Bass' farm was nearby, the settlement was named for him.

Shortly after the passing of his first wife in 1871, Bass married Sarah Hogg, with whom he fathered two more children. Eventually, as the years passed, the community of Bass faded with the closing of the mercantile, and Bass, having reached his advancing years, went to live with his daughter.

When he died in 1920 at the impressive age of ninety-eight, he was believed to be the oldest resident of Cole County and was interred in Hickory Hill Cemetery. Of the eight children he and his two wives raised, one of Bass' sons would carry on the tradition of a life defined by intriguing experiences.

John Perry "J.P." Bass was born in the settlement of Bass on September 14, 1848. A history shared by Palmer Scheperle in the book, *History of the Scheperle Family of America*, explained that J.P. Bass fell in love with Mary Scheperle, whose family had settled in and around the communities of Stringtown and Millbrook.

"The couple was not of legal age, and Mary did not have her parents' permission to marry John Bass, a Methodist," Palmer Scheperle explained. "They persuaded the Justice of the Peace that they were of legal age and then eloped on horseback," he added.

Through his marriage to Scheperle in 1868, Bass became the brother-in-law of John Scheperle Sr., a co-founder of the Centennial Mill in Millbrook. Scheperle Sr. was also the individual responsible for overseeing the construction of St. John's Lutheran Church in Stringtown and Immanuel Lutheran Church in Honey Creek. Even after his marriage to a Lutheran woman, he raised his family in the Methodist denomination. Although it is not documented whether continued tensions existed between Bass and his wife's family because of his faith, he made the decision to start anew in a community away from his in-laws by moving his family to Texas in 1878.

"John and Mary owned extensive property in and around Mineral Wells and in Wise and Hall County, Texas," the Scheperle book clarified. "The Bass family were cotton farmers, owning a cotton gin, and raised cattle in Wise and Hall Counties."

Mary gave birth to three children—one son and two daughters—while they still lived in the farm community of Bass, but they were raised to adulthood in Texas. Like his father, John suffered the tragedy of losing his first wife, who died in 1905—the same year her brother was building St. John's Lutheran Church in Stringtown. The body of Bass' fifty-four-year-old wife was buried in a cemetery in Newlin, Texas.

Newspaper records indicate that J.P. Bass returned to Mid-Missouri sometime after his wife's death and in 1910 married Sarah Lumpkin in Miller County. Her first husband, Esom Lumpkin, had died in 1900. At the time of her marriage to Bass, she had two children that were independent adults.

"Roscoe Lumpkin and wife came in Tuesday to visit their mother, Mrs. J.P. Bass, at Spring Garden," the *Miller County Autogram-Sentinel* printed on September 22, 1910.

A week later, another newspaper explained that Bass was preparing for his return to Texas with his second wife.

"Mr. and Mrs. J.P. Bass shipped some household goods from here Saturday to Memphis, Texas . . . [and] will go from Jefferson City about Tuesday . . . where they expect to make their home in the future," the *Eldon Advertiser* reported on September 29, 1910.

J.P. Bass and his wife traveled to Missouri on several occasions to visit family and attend funerals, including the burial of Metheldred Bass Sr. in 1920. They lived to witness the disappearance of the settlement of Bass, a decline beginning with the closing of the mercantile that had defined the community.

In 1936, J.P. Bass died at eighty-seven years of age, and services were held at the local Methodist church followed by burial in a cemetery in Memphis, Texas. His second wife died six years later and was laid to rest alongside him.

Old Bass Road now stretches between U.S. Highway 54 and State Route AA, providing only a road sign to designate the legacy of a bygone community and the dissipating history of the Bass family in southern Cole County. The pioneer who inspired the naming of Bass, Missouri, is no longer living, but his gravestone in Hickory Hill Cemetery is a hidden reminder of the contribution he made to our local rural tapestry.

In the words of writer Henry S.F. Cooper, "A man who thinks too much about his ancestors is like a potato—the best part of him is underground."

Burials do not end the story of pioneer families. The Bass name is etched on the tombstones in several quiet country cemeteries but may someday inspire others to delve into the history of those whose sacrifices provided for the betterment of their families and communities. *(Photographs courtesy of Palmer Scheperle.)*

__Martin Luther Scrivner – Russellville__

Only days after turning eight years old in 1892, Martin Luther Scrivner lost his father, a Union veteran of the Civil War. This early distress was supplemented two years later when he was orphaned by the passing of his mother. This began an unfortunate period of unsettlement, resulting in his desire to establish something that he had been denied in his youth—a complete family circle.

After the passing of his parents, both of whom were laid to rest in Enloe Cemetery near Russellville, Martin was placed in the care of his older half-brother, John Enoch Scrivner.

"He received a pension for his father's service in the military until the age of sixteen," wrote Doris Scrivner Collier in *The Descendants of Benjamin Scrivner* —a self-published family history. The book further explained, "He moved to Oklahoma with John's family and returned to Missouri and lived with his sister, Kate, until his marriage."

Cole County marriage records reveal that a twenty-two-year-old Martin Scrivner was living in Russellville when he married his fiancée, Birdie Jane Sappenfield, at the bygone community of Bass on September 2, 1906.

The former Birdie Jane Sappenfield grew up in the community of Scrivner, named for Martin Luther Scrivner's half-brother. She and Martin married in 1906.

Prior to their marriage, Birdie Sappenfield was a resident of the community of Scrivner, once located a few miles south of Russellville. It was a settlement founded in the early 1880s by John Scrivner, the half-brother who helped raise young Martin after he was orphaned. Sappenfield was also a niece of John Scrivner's wife, Nancy.

"John sold groceries from his house for a time; then he built a general store," explained Sharon Brown, Marie Strobel, and Delores Twitchel in a narrative printed in Russellville's sesquicentennial book from 1988.

"Next, he added a blacksmith shop across the road. Soon he put a post office in the back of the store," the book continued. "The store sold not only groceries but also material, jewelry, dishes, shoes, all types of clothing, and hardware."

Regardless of the assorted business opportunities available in the once-booming community of Scrivner, Martin chose to suspend any mercantile interests and embark upon his married life while pursuing the same type of work that had been embraced by his late father.

"The first place they lived was on a farm several miles south of Russellville on State Route AA near the [Miller County] line," said Janie Jones, granddaughter of Martin and Birdie. "My mother, Marcella, was the youngest and she was born on the farm," she added.

The couple raised five children, eventually choosing to leave the farming lifestyle and pursue a different path in the nearby community of Russellville. Martin and Birdie purchased a house in the south section of town, which placed them near the building where they would engage in a business interest.

"Having sold our grocery business in Russellville to Martin L. Scrivner, who will assume charge of the same next Monday, we take this means of extending thanks to our many friends who have favored us with their patronage during the past two years," wrote John and Lydia Smith regarding the sale of their store in a clipping from the July 30, 1936, edition of the *Central Missourian*.

"In turning over the business to Mr. Scrivner, a man of high principle and honesty, who is well known to you, we trust that you will give him the same liberal and courteous patronage you have given us."

Martin operated the store for many years in downtown Russellville in partnership with his son, Foster, who had previous business experience as owner of a café in Jefferson City. In the early 1940s, Martin sold the store after Foster moved his family to the St. Louis area to pursue his newfound trade as a machinist.

"At some point, my grandparents moved into a two-story house north of Russellville on Rockhouse Road," said Jane Jones. "After my grandfather sold the grocery store in town, he went to work at the nearby MFA Exchange and I recall my grandmother talking about how Grandpa would walk to and from work every day."

The Scrivner family, Jones noted, were raised as Baptists. Her mother, Marcella, was baptized a member of the Cole Spring Baptist Church west of town. In later years, Jones went on to explain, she spent additional time with her grandparents because of a medical situation.

"My mother had the mumps in 1954 or so, and we went to stay with my grandparents in Russellville," Jones said. "My brother, Jerry [Koestner] was a baby at the time and because my mom was bedridden, my grandmother helped take care of us and would feed Jerry with a bottle, I remember."

Jones said that her grandfather later developed Alzheimer's and died on May 30, 1957, when seventy-three years old. His wife, Birdie, died at ninety-six years of age in 1980 and was laid to rest alongside her husband in Mt. Carmel Cemetery near Brazito, the final resting site of many of their relatives.

Although only ten years old when her grandfather passed away, Jones finds solace in the few memories from the time they spent together and the creation of moments that provided peace to a man who endured great hardships in his early years.

"In the end, when my grandfather was suffering from Alzheimer's, he would either sit in his chair or just lay in bed, and my grandmother had to take care of him," she said. "But I know one thing for sure—he was a good and dedicated family man before he fell ill and he and his wife were able to raise many wonderful children together. I just wish that I had been given the time to get to

know him better but I am grateful for what memories we shared."
(Photographs courtesy of Jane Jones.)

William "Dave" and Polly Ann (Allee) Hader – Mt. Herman

Of the thousands of German immigrants that flooded into the
United States during the nineteenth century, many established homes
in Central Missouri. It was there that they discovered opportunities
in agriculture and built a legacy and interest in farming often handed
down to their children. The stories they brought with them from
overseas—and those created by their offspring—offer a fascinating
glimpse into the fabric of local rural history and family surnames that
were once quite prevalent.

"Jacob Hader is our forefather that came to America," wrote
Helen Atkinson in the late 1970s. In her writings, Atkinson explained
that her mother, Mettie Serl, who was the granddaughter of Jacob,

requested that she begin collecting information on the lineage of the Hader family "for future posterity."

"It is to my sorrow that I did not start earlier as my mother passed away October 1, 1979," Atkinson added.

Her research, most of which can be confirmed by census documents, notes that Jacob Hader was born in Switzerland on August 17, 1824, but spent many of his formative years in Germany. As a young man, he made the decision to become a Catholic priest but later, for reasons unknown to his descendants, left the seminary.

"His father was said to be very mean to him," Atkinson continued. "He came across [to the United States] with friends, the Latshaw family, and came to America at an early age. We do not know his parents' names."

Mettie Serl, far left, is pictured with her sisters. Mettie asked her daughter in 1978 to collect information about her grandfather, Jacob Hader. Sadly, Mettie passed away the following year. Courtesy of Charles Jobe.

After arriving in the mid-1840s, he met Susanah Myers, who was described as "Pennsylvania Dutch" and living in the vicinity of California, Missouri. The couple married on January 6, 1846, and settled on a farm in Miller County near Eldon, where they went on to raise twelve children.

Jacob Hader was fifty-six years old when he passed away on May 22, 1881, and was laid to rest in Dooley Cemetery near Eldon. His widow later lived with their son, William David Hader, for many years until her death in 1897.

"William David Hader was my great-grandfather, but I never met him because he died before I was born," said Charles Jobe. "I've always wished I would have had that opportunity," he added.

Born in Miller County in 1854, William "David" Hader was the fifth oldest of Jacob and Susanah's twelve children. On September 2, 1862, he wedded Polly Ann Allee, and they together raised seven children. The Hader family became members of the Baptist denomination, and family documents indicate David Hader transferred his membership from Flag Springs Baptist Church to Mt. Herman Baptist Church in Miller County in 1897. For many years, he served as a deacon and was later a member of Enon Baptist Church prior to transferring back to the Mt. Herman congregation.

The October 27, 1904, edition of the *Eldon Advertiser* shared notice of the program for an upcoming meeting involving the congregation of which Hader was an active member. According to the newspaper, "Program of the meeting, of the Ministers and Deacons, of the Miller County Baptist Association, to be held with the Mt. Herman Church beginning Friday evening . . ." The article added, "7:00 p.m. Devotional service, led by David Hader."

The *Eldon Advertiser* printed on December 31, 1914, that Hader's daughter, Pearl Hader, married Mr. Henry Rea. The newspaper said of Pearl, "The bride is the daughter Wm. Hader, one of our best citizens. Mr. Hader lives just across the line in Moniteau County, but we claim him as our own citizen."

Five years later, in 1919, when a crowd gathered at Mt. Herman Baptist Church for the funeral of John D. Kaufman of Olean, a fellow farmer, David Hader made a heartfelt speech that helped provide comfort to the family in mourning.

Charles Jobe explained, "They lived in a log cabin that they built on their farm east of what is now Highway FF but south of County Line Road [southeast of Enon]. They later moved the cabin down County Line Road—on the same farm—and it became part of a new house."

Linda (Enloe) Amick, a great-granddaughter of David Hader, also never had the opportunity to meet her relative. But through stories shared by her mother, the former Marble Roth, she was able to learn much about the late farmer and Baptist deacon.

"As I was told, he supposedly had a special gift he exercised through prayer," Amick said. "Apparently, if someone had an animal that was ill or if someone in their family had been stricken by an illness, they would contact David Hader to pray for them, and the animal or person often regained their health."

Charles Jobe explained that his grandfather, Charles Serl, left a good job with General Motors in St. Louis to return to rural Cole County to help take care of his wife's parents, David and Polly Ann Hader, in their golden years. Polly Ann passed away in 1934 and was laid to rest in Allen Cemetery near Olean; three years later, her husband, David, joined her in eternal rest approximately two weeks after his eighty-third birthday.

In the context of countless immigrants who departed their homelands in Germany and surrounding regions to make the journey to the U.S. in the nineteenth century, the story of Jacob Hader is not abundantly unique. However, his experiences are a testament to the visionaries who found their way to Missouri, establishing new lives and inspiring their offspring to carry forth a farming legacy.

"My family never really told any stories about Jacob Hader or his son, David, and I waited way too long to try and find something out about them because those who would know are now gone," said Charle Jobe. "These immigrant families were important in that they built farms and legacies that would last for generations. Thankfully, his granddaughter had the foresight to share what she knew of the families of Jacob and David so that we could have some insight into their lives," he added. *(Photograph courtesy of Linda (Enloe) Amick.)*

Dr. Clark S. Glover – Russellville

Clark S. Glover was born near Russellville in 1874 and was no stranger to hard work, toiling on local farms in the spring and summer months while attending school in the winter. His professional career began as a teacher at a school near Enon prior to enrolling in the American Medical College in St. Louis. Dr. Glover became established in Russellville in 1901 when he purchased the medical practice of Dr. Tom Short. His office was located in the former Schubert's Liquor Store - a small brick building that has been remodeled and is still being used for a small business. Eventually, Dr. Glover made enough money to purchase a horse and buggy and later a car, using the vehicle to visit patients throughout areas in the counties of Cole, Miller, and Moniteau.

At the time he was practicing medicine, there was no ambulance service, and in case of an emergency, the patient was often loaded on the train in Russellville and transported to the hospital in Jefferson City on the Bagnell Branch of the Missouri Pacific Railroad. In addition to his medical practice, Dr. Glover remained active in Democratic politics, was a member of the local Masonic Lodge, served as Cole County Health Officer, and was vice-president of the Community Bank of Russellville. His younger brother, Tandy, graduated from the same medical class in 1901 and went on to serve the citizens of the Eugene community as a physician for many years while also working on his own farm. Their sister, Cynthia, married John Scheperle Jr. of Millbrook, who built the parsonage of St. John's Lutheran Church in Stringtown and moved Centennial Mill from Millbrook to Lohman in 1906.

In the fall of 1920, it was reported that nearly all of Russellville showed up at the Circuit Court in Jefferson City as either spectators or witnesses in the suit filed by John B. Endicott against Emmett Robertson. Apparently, Endicott, who was at the time the principal of Russellville School, used a hickory switch on one of Robertson's sons who was being unruly in class. As the November 17, 1920, edition of the *Daily Capital News* reported, it was alleged that "Robertson took the teacher to task for treatment of his child . . ." According to *The Heritage of Russellville in Cole County*, "Endicott testified that Robertson followed him to a garage and knocked him down several times. Dr. Glover was brought into court to testify that the educator's face was badly battered. Robertson was fined $20 "and costs" in the assault.

Dr. Clark Glover sold his practice in 1936 due to failing health and purchased a two-hundred-acre farm near Russellville. He is reputed to have been a staunch Baptist and was a member of the historic Cole Springs Baptist Church for a number of years before helping establish the Russellville Baptist Church in 1903. The sixty-nine-year-old physician passed away at his home in Russellville in January 1943 and was laid to rest in nearby Enloe Cemetery. His wife, Estella Bond, died in 1965 and lies at rest next to him. *(Photograph courtesy of Jim and Eve Campbell.)*

John and Grace (Hader) Selix – Olean

"One day, we will all cherish the memory of having blacksmiths on every corner," *penned American author George Singleton. This powerful quote describes individuals such as the late John Franklin Selix, who for years worked in a trade that was never fully appreciated but provided a crucial service in the small communities where he resided.*

John Selix's lineage traces from his grandfather, James Selix, who immigrated to the United States from Germany and initially settled in Pennsylvania during the 1840s.

According to the research of the late Pauline Selix, ". . . James went to the 'California Gold Rush' from Pittsburg in 1849. He would have been about 22 years old." She continued, "After finding some gold, he seemed to have gotten back as far as Maysville [Missouri] and bought a farm west of town. In 1856, James married a local girl, Julia Ann Morgan. James served in the Union Army during the Civil War."

NEW BLACKSMITH SHOP

Now Open for Business

We wish to announce to the public in general that we have opened up a blacksmith shop in the Steffens Building, just south of the Farmers' Shipping Association, and solicit a portion of your blacksmith and woodwork, assuring you that all our work will be strictly first class and prices will be reasonable.

We have had years of experience in this line of work and feel that we are prepared to care for your wants in a prompt and satisfactory manner. Your patronage will be appreciated.

Campbell & Selix
Russellville, Mo.

After closing his blacksmith shop in Decatur in 1921, Selix and Campbell advertised their new partnership in Russellville. Courtesy of Eve Campbell

James and his first wife (who died in 1867 when only 30 years old) had two sons—Frank and Simeon. It was in 1884 that Simeon married Nancy Shadwick and the couple later moved to a farm near Olean in Miller County. They went on to raise five children, the second to youngest being John Franklin Selix, born in 1890.

In October 1911, John Selix married Grace Hader, whose father, William "David," was a farmer in the Olean area, deacon in a small Baptist church, and a well-respected member of the community.

"They set up housekeeping in the village of Decatur south of Russellville," wrote the late Orville "Jack" Selix about his parents.

Decatur, once a thriving settlement, disappeared decades ago but was located along the South Moreau Creek and boasted a post office, hotel, mill, and other small businesses and homes.

Jack continued, "Both Ladean [his sister] and I were born there. My dad did blacksmithing most of his life."

Living in Decatur helped introduce Selix to two individuals that played pivotal roles in his career as a blacksmith. First, the mill in the community was owned by Gustave N. Steffens, the son of a German immigrant and a person possessing great business acumen and mercantile interests. Secondly, while living in Decatur, Selix met a fellow blacksmith who became a lifelong friend, Otto Campbell.

"When I was about six years old, my folks rented a house in Russellville, which they later bought," Jack explained. "Mother always had a good garden and did home canning . . . We lived at the end of the street and had a cow and chicken," he added.

With the town of Russellville enjoying the economic benefit of the railroad passing through downtown, the decision to leave Decatur was made by several business owners during this period of time.

A newspaper of the era, *The Cole County Weekly*, reported on December 9, 1921, "Otto Campbell of this place [Russellville] and John Selix, former blacksmith at Decatur, will open up a blacksmith shop at this place Thursday. They will be located in the shed of G.N. Steffens, across from the Farmer's Poultry House."

Jack also noted that his father, when not engaged in his black-smithing responsibilities, embraced opportunities to raise saddle horses and engage in a little "horse trading." Other times, Selix made money by using his horses as breeding stock.

"Otto Campbell and John Selix have obtained a fine dark iron gray Percheron stallion, which they will keep here this season for breeding purposes," printed the *Central Missourian* on February 25, 1937. "This horse is a very fine animal, weighs, around 1,700 pounds, and is well built."

Several months after their move to Russellville, Selix and Campbell built an addition to their blacksmith shop to handle the increased workload. Their blacksmithing duties included making tools and shoeing horses, while also fashioning and repairing implements and other equipment used by the local farmers.

Selix and Campbell remained in partnership throughout the next few years although there were brief moments in their blacksmithing careers when they chose to work solo. During the early 1930s, Selix split from Campbell and operated a blacksmith business in the community of Olean. In 1936, Selix again joined Campbell in business in Russellville, purchased a warehouse building, and had it moved downtown to use as their new blacksmith shop. However, as Jack Selix explained, Campbell fell ill, and the decision was made to close the shop.

"Dad went to work sharpening steel on the Mississippi River," Jack Selix wrote. "Mother and I rented a house in Eldon and I finished high school there . . . Later Grandmother Selix passed away and Dad and Mother bought the Selix farm from the heirs."

Charles Jobe added, "My parents would take us to see my Great Uncle Selix when I was a kid, and they lived on the Selix farm a few miles south of Enon. From what I remember, he had the abilities (sic) to fix about anything."

John Selix's beloved wife, Grace, passed away in 1958 and the retired blacksmith decided to move to the Kansas City area two years later to live with his daughter. Following his death in 1962 at the age of seventy-one, he was interred alongside his wife at Allen Cemetery near Olean.

The impact John Selix had as a blacksmith—a near-forgotten profession—in the communities where he lived and worked is nearly impossible to measure, although his toils often kept others operating in their own line of work. Yet it was not just his work, but his commitment to family that earned him praise regarding the influence he and his wife had on the lives of their children.

With sincerity and heartfelt reflection, Jack Selix wrote, "Dad and Mother were both hard workers and always supported Ladean and I (sic) . . . and taught us to be good citizens by their example." *(Photograph courtesy of Charles Jobe.)*

Otto and Elza (Roark) Campbell – Russellville

There are those in history who are remembered not only because of their profession but the associations and friendships they maintained. Otto Campbell, a native of the Russellville area, can be categorized as such, having earned the distinction as a talented and capable blacksmith who spent much of his life in business with his close friend, John Selix.

Born in 1895 and raised on a farm in the northern section of Russellville, Otto was the oldest of two sons and two daughters born to James W. and Polly Campbell. Their home, located near the Bagnell Branch of the Missouri Pacific Railroad, provided a business hub that introduced him to tradesmen like J.W. Amos and Hubert Brumbach, both of whom were wagon-makers and blacksmiths.

Little is known about Campbell's early years other than he was employed in some capacity for the Missouri Pacific Railroad but

Otto is pictured as an infant in 1896 with his parents, James and Polly (Steenbergen) Campbell. Courtesy of Jim and Eve Campbell

later began to learn black-smithing under the tutelage of local shop owners. On August 17, 1913, he married Elza M. Roark, also a native of the Russellville community.

"Otto Campbell, black-smith at the Brumbach shop at this place [Russellville] suffered a slight scalp wound last Saturday when he was struck on the head by a fractious mule, which he was attempting to shoe," reported the *Central Missouri Leader* on February 4, 1921.

Though still a young man, Campbell had refined his blacksmithing abilities to the extent that only a few months later, he resigned his position with Brumbach and entered a business partnership with a man that would remain a consistent part of his life for years to come.

"NEW BLACKSMITH SHOP," the bold headline read in the newspaper printed by the *Central Missouri Leader* on December 9, 1921. The paper further explained, "Otto Campbell and (John) F. Selix have purchased the blacksmith equipment of Robert Scott, at Elston and are moving the same to Russellville where they will open a shop in the Steffens building just south of the Farmers Shipping Association."

The twenty-six-year-old Campbell and his partner, Selix, were described as "good workmen with years of experience."

The blacksmithing duo would build their business through-out the next several years while also partnering in the purchase of fine horses to be used for breeding. But in 1929, Campbell severed his business relationship with Selix when he went to work for the Eberhart Brothers Garage in Russellville.

In the years following his marriage, Otto and his wife became parents to three sons and three daughters; sadly, one daughter died when only seven years old. The family was also actively involved in the local community and were members of the Russellville Baptist Church. In the early 1930s, as the Great Depression was beginning to evolve, Campbell re-opened his blacksmith shop in Russellville. In 1934, he posted an advertisement in the local newspaper urging those in the community that were indebted to him, to settle their accounts so that he could in turn meet his obligations.

"There was an old-timer from the area that told me several years ago that Otto survived the Great Depression by bartering," said Jim Campbell, Otto's grandson. "A lot of people didn't have the money to pay for his blacksmith services, so he would trade out his work for things he and his family needed," he added.

As a blacksmith, Campbell was often called upon to employ his skills to make unique repairs for his friends and neighbors.

"August Heidbreder was having the furnace of his molasses machinery repaired at the Campbell Blacksmith shop the first of the week and will again try his luck at manufacturing old-time Missouri sorghum," the Central Missourian shared on September 27, 1934.

By the spring of 1936, John Selix, who had for the past several years been operating a blacksmith shop in Olean, renewed his partnership with Campbell in Russellville.

"One story Grandpa Otto told my father was that their shop was across the street from Dr. Glover's house," said Jim Campbell. "When the doctor came in at night, he'd hang his pants on the banister at the bottom of the stairs (inside the front door) in case he had to leave on a call in the middle of the night."

"He had done this one night after coming in from his office next door and later that evening, someone snuck in and stole his pants, which had all of his money in it (sic)."

Campbell continued to operate his breeding stables for saddle stallions and worked with Selix in purchasing high-class horses for this business endeavor. But as Jack Selix, the son of Campbell's long-time partner, wrote in later years, Campbell became ill and the blacksmith shop was closed.

His health was never fully restored but Campbell worked the last two years of his life at the Ozark Lumber Company in Russellville. According to his obituary, the fifty-three-year-old retired blacksmith suffered a fatal heart attack while at work on March 8, 1948. Following the funeral services, he was laid to rest in nearby Enloe Cemetery.

Jim Campbell, who was born many years after his grandfather's death, has come to know him by stories passed down through relatives and community members. Much of what he has been told highlights the significance of Otto Campbell's chosen profession.

"Otto was well known in this community because of his abilities as a blacksmith and, years ago, if you mentioned blacksmiths in Russellville, the old-timers thought you were speaking about Otto." He continued, "People used to ask me if I was related to Otto, and when I said yes, they'd reply, 'He was one heck of a blacksmith.' Blacksmiths were the mechanics of their day—true craftsmen." (Photographs courtesy of Jim and Eve Campbell.)

Henry Weber – Millbrook

Throughout the years, Mark Weber heard many fascinating tales about his great uncle, Henry Weber, who was wounded in World War I and laid in a trench before being discovered by a fellow soldier. Time has ways of embellishing such stories, but research has helped confirm aspects of this heroic moment, providing members of the family with insight into a long-deceased relative.

Born on a farm near Millbrook (south of Lohman) on March 17, 1894, Henry Weber was one of twelve children of Carl and Elizabeth Weber. His grandparents had emigrated from Germany years earlier, bringing with them a few traditions that included their Christian faith.

"All of the family were members of St. Paul's Lutheran Church in Lohman," explained Mark Weber.

According to a 110th anniversary booklet produced by St. Paul's in 1962, Henry Weber was among eleven young individuals confirmed in 1907. As a young man, he attended school at a local one-room schoolhouse and received two years of parochial education in the German school once located at St. Paul's Lutheran Church.

Weber married the former Minnie Doehla in 1921 at St. Paul's Lutheran Church in Lohman. Courtesy of Mark Weber

On June 5, 1917, the twenty-three-year-old was working as a farmer in the Millbrook area when he complied with the Selective Service Act. He participated in the first of three draft registrations of World War I, which "was for all men between the ages of 21 and 31," noted an article from the National Archives.

His draft order number was soon drawn and on September 20, 1917, Weber was inducted into the U.S. Army and sent to Camp Funston, Kansas, to begin training with the 89th Infantry Division.

"The 89th Infantry Division can . . . claim to typify the best results of the mighty effort made by the United States to put into the field an efficient fighting force in the minimum time," explained the *History of the 89th Division*. The book added, "Drawn from the great Middle West, its composition was largely that of the native born, agriculture class . . . most truly representative of American traditions and ideals."

Assigned to Company M, 356th Infantry, Weber initially served with soldiers predominantly drawn from northwest Missouri. Throughout the next several months, the Mid-Missouri farmer was forged into a soldier, learning to use machine guns and similar weapons while being immersed in the principles of trench warfare that defined combat on the Western Front.

The soldiers of the division were lined up along both sides of a road on November 26, 1917, where their commander, Major General Leonard Wood, passed through on his way to the station prior to departing for France for observation duty. As the *History of the 89th Division* explained, the "Division was constantly being made and re-made. Large contingents of men equipped and partially trained in Camp Funston were sent to fill deficiencies in other divisions which were supposed to be destined for earlier service overseas . . ."

In the spring of 1918, Private Weber became one of these replacements when reassigned to Company G, 4th Infantry Regiment of the 3rd Infantry Division. On April 6, 1918, he departed the United States aboard the transport *USS Great Northern* at Newport News, Virginia. After arriving in France, Weber and the soldiers of the 4th Infantry soon received their baptism by fire.

"On July 14, 1918, units of the Third (Division) were assigned a 12-kilometer line along the Marne River from Chateau-Thierry to Varennes," wrote Jeffrey Gaul in *History of the Third Infantry Division*. He added, "Their section was not ready for a major assault." The book continued, "According to records, the 3rd Div. lost nearly 8,000 men during the course of the Marne defensive, but the German defensive was even worse . . . The Third once again proved itself by helping to throw back a major German offensive at Chateau-Thierry and other vital points along the Marne that could have resulted in the capture of Paris."

The division earned the name "Rock of the Marne" for their remarkable performance in the face of overwhelming odds, but not without sacrifice. In addition to those killed, records denote that Weber was seriously wounded when shot through the lower thigh of his right leg on July 28, 1918.

Mark Weber explained, "I remember my father saying that his uncle laid in a trench for three days before he was found by someone."

The soldier spent several months in a hospital in France recovering from his wound. Transport records from World War I indicate he was assigned to a convalescent detachment in Bordeaux, France, when he left Europe aboard the SS Sierra on February 19, 1919. The ship was packed with soldiers who incurred a variety of wounds, injuries, and illnesses. Returning to the U.S. in early March 1919, Weber was soon discharged and returned to farming for the next several years. He married the former Minnie Doehla of Lohman in 1921, with whom he raised a son and a daughter.

In 1939, the couple moved to Russellville, where Weber worked as a painter and carpenter. They eventually moved to Jefferson City in 1958, where the veteran passed away in 1971 when seventy-seven years old. A member of Trinity Lutheran Church in Russellville at the time of his death, he is interred in Hawthorn Memorial Gardens.

For years, Mark Weber listened as his family shared vague retellings of his great uncle's combat experiences, never able to verify the accuracy of the astonishing accounts.

"My father would always say that my great uncle walked with a limp and then shared with us the World War I story, saying he was wounded and laid in a trench for three days until someone came across him," Mark Weber said. He added, "I never really knew my great uncle, but it's nice to be able to find out more about his service and confirm he was injured in combat." *(Photographs courtesy of Mark Weber.)*

Eliga Norfleet – Brazito

Brazito is a community bursting with stories of people who earned the respect of their peers and made a decent living without taking advantage of others. This once bustling area, for many decades, benefitted from a spirited resident known by many as "Lige," who not only repaired small engines for a nominal charge but helped expand and maintain the local phone system while remaining dedicated to his Christian faith. Born on January 22, 1909, on a farm southwest of Brazito near a defunct community known as Bass, Eliga David Norfleet acquired an early interest in the agricultural lifestyle while working on a farm established by his great-grandfather.

In 1964, when his shop in Brazito was soon to be torn down for the expansion of Highway 54, Norfleet built this circular shop on his nearby farm. Courtesy of Naomi Cox

"He had four sisters and his father died when he was only sixteen years old, so he more or less had to help take care of the family," said Naomi Cox, Norfleet's daughter and only child.

She continued, "He attended the one-room Mt. Union School and in 1936, married my mother (Oneta Busch). We all lived on the family farm and my father also worked several years for his father-in-law, Norman Busch, at the general store he owned along the old two-lane Highway 54 in Brazito," she added.

Norfleet, who was recognized by his neighbors and members of the community as a hard worker, also invested many hours on his family's farm planting and harvesting crops in addition to raising livestock.

Cox said, "I can remember us putting out a huge garden every year and picking dozens of gallons of blackberries that we then sold."

When his father-in-law sold the store and moved to Eldon, Norfleet continued working for the new owner, Clarence Angerer. But as his daughter recalls, he decided to pursue a new career by attending classes in Eldon and earning a certificate for working on small engines and equipment.

He then rented a shop from local farmer Fred "Fritz" Hirshman located just east of the Angerer General Store in Brazito. It was in this small building that he began to ply his new trade by working on chainsaws and lawnmowers for local residents and those passing through the area on Highway 54.

"For some time, he worked out of that small building in Brazito until the mid-1960s," said Cox. "Somehow, he heard that the highway department had plans to widen Highway 54 into four lanes and it would come through where his shop was sitting."

A photograph Cox shared shows her father beginning construction of a new shop on his farm on Old Bass Road in 1964. Unlike his previous building in Brazito, Norfleet embraced a unique design feature for his new shop.

"The building was round, and he told me that he did that because he didn't want to be able to stack junk in the corners," chuckled his nephew, Ron Busch. "Uncle Lige was also a devout Christian and it seemed like anytime the church door was open at Hickory Hill (Baptist Church), he was there."

Busch also explained that his uncle, though able to repair riding mowers, was hesitant to work on such equipment for the younger ones in his extended family.

"I had taken a riding mower by his shop to have it fixed and it just sat there," Busch said. "After a while, I asked my dad why Uncle Lige wasn't working on it, and he told me that he didn't think that I needed it and could use a push mower for cutting my grass."

Family, church, small-scale farming, and equipment repair represented a full slate of daily activities. However, Norfleet also found time to volunteer on the board of nearby Spring Garden Cemetery and served as president of the Eugene Telephone Company.

"As a kid, I can remember him wearing these cleats on his shoes so that he could climb telephone poles and help take care of the lines," said Naomi Cox. "He carried some type of ringer with him that he hooked to the lines and spoke to someone to make sure everything was working properly."

Many from the Brazito area recall that Norfleet had little trouble getting their equipment back in top operating condition and charged very little to do so, which resulted in a steady stream of customers for his small business.

"When he got older, he slowed down a little and began to fall behind on his repair work, so he had my two sons help him in the shop to catch up," Cox said. "But they grew older and moved on, and eventually were no longer around to help him."

Cox also noted that when she moved to the Eldon area, her parents transferred their membership from Hickory Hill and began attending the Ninth Street Christian Church.

The passing of years reduced some of her father's early vigor, but Norfleet never fully retired and continued to work on projects until his death. He was eighty-two years old when he died in 1991 and is buried in Spring Garden Cemetery, the final resting site he for years helped maintain. His wife passed away in 2002 and is interred with him.

The farm now belongs to a different family and both repair shops he used in his career have been torn down, yet memories of the departed repairman live on through recollections of friends and family from the Brazito area.

"He would always tease the kids when they came in the shop with their parents, but in a fun way that many of us recall with joyful reflection," said Cox.

Norfleet's nephew, Ron Busch, added, "He was kind of a loner because he was always busy working on small engines, but everybody knew and respected him because he was a Christian, was good at working on things, and never overcharged." *(Photographs courtesy of Naomi Cox.)*

John Edward "Eddie" Loesch – Zion Community

John Edward "Eddie" Loesch, along with two brothers and a sister, grew up on a farm southwest of the Zion community, learning early in their lives the value of hard work and family. They would be confirmed at nearby Zion Lutheran Church and, when World War II erupted, Eddie Loesch was well into adulthood when called into the service. Years later, his niece would come to enjoy the memories of the time spent with her uncle, but never fully comprehending the turmoil he carried as a result of injuries that he sustained during the war.

"My Uncle Eddie was a very interesting person and attended the parochial school at Zion and the old one-room Corinth School while growing up," said Candace Stockton. "When it came to the military, he never really talked about his service," she added. "I know that he received a Purple Heart and some other medals, but I never knew much more than that."

John "Eddie" Loesch grew up on a farm near the Zion community. He was working as a bricklayer when he was inducted into the Army in World War II. While serving overseas, he was injured and earned a Purple Heart medal.

Like many of his contemporaries, Loesch fell within the age group of those required to register with their local draft board in 1941. The following year, on April 8, 1942, he was inducted into the U.S. Army at Jefferson Barracks in St. Louis, where he received his uniforms, aptitude tests, and inoculations. Having set aside the tools he used as a bricklayer to serve his nation, Loesch's introduction to active-duty service began with basic training at Fort Leonard Wood. He then went on to complete advanced training as a small-arms weapons mechanic.

Seventeen months of stateside service came to an end when he departed the U.S. on November 3, 1944. Arriving in Europe nine days later, he was assigned to the 137th Ordnance Company and began utilizing his maintenance skills in support of the war effort.

"Mechanics of the 137th Ordnance Company, a heavy maintenance unit supporting troops of Lt. Gen. Jacob L. Devers' 6th Army Group, have combined skill and ingenuity to operate an Army 'assembly line' factory that gets damaged material back on the line and new material 'fighting fit' for combat," reported the *Berwyn Life* (Berwyn, Illinois) on March 21, 1945. The newspaper continued, "The ordnance men also process new artillery pieces, small arms, fire control instruments, and such combat vehicles as armored cars, readying them for their first combat. A vehicle will hit six different shops for an overall check and emerge complete even to ammunition for its weapons."

The Chattanooga Daily Times on March 18, 1945, noted of Loesch and his fellow soldiers, "The unit's experts are so versatile that they are able to repair almost any instrument of war coming their way."

This mission, though critical to the war effort, did not place Loesch on the front lines of combat; however, it also did not remove them from the dangers present in a war zone.

"I remember it being talked about that my Uncle Eddie was driving a Jeep overseas and hit a land mine," recalled Candace Stockton. "Apparently it killed everyone riding in it except him, and his injuries were such that he had to be taken to the hospital."

Military records indicate that Loesch was removed from the combat

Loesch became a confirmed member at Zion Lutheran Church in 1920.

zone and sent back to the states on March 16, 1945, after incur-
ring injuries that earned him a Purple Heart. He was transferred to
the Hospital Center at Camp Carson, Colorado, where after several
months of recovery, he was discharged from the U.S. Army on July
30, 1945.

"When he came home from the service, I was only about five
years old, but I remember that he had to use a cane to walk," Candace
Stockton recalled. "In later years, he was able to get rid of the cane
but always walked with a limp."

Loesch returned to his pre-war employment as a bricklayer,
earning the reputation as being one of the most competent and able
in this trade in Central Missouri. Although he had girlfriends in the
years following his service, he never married nor had any children.
Instead, he chose to live with his parents and help them around the
farm as they entered their golden years. Carrying the burden of hidden wounds of war, Loesch often found solace through fishing and
hunting trips and enjoyed the company of his fellow veterans and
friends from the community.

"Nine hunters climbed aboard a converted school bus and left
Friday for 10 days of deer hunting in southwest Colorado," noted
the *Sunday News and Tribune* on October 16, 1960. With Loesch
counted among this group, the newspaper added, "If successful,
they'll cure the meat and strap it to a special rack atop the bus for the
return trip."

Sifting through dozens of photographs, Candace Stockton
pointed to one and remarked, "Here's one of him with several deer,
so they were often successful."

As the years passed, Loesch was occasionally afflicted with
memories of military service, his injuries, and the deaths of fellow
soldiers. Too often relying upon alcohol for relief, he was only seventy-one years old when he passed away in 1978 and was laid to rest in
the cemetery of Zion Lutheran Church.

For Candace Stockton, her childhood and youth are filled with many good memories of time spent with her uncle and have imbued in her a deep and abiding respect for the sacrifice he made for his country.

"Growing up, I was around him often because he lived next door and would come over for meals a lot and visits—we were really a close family," Stockton said. "But I have always been curious about his military service because there were so many questions that I would have loved to have asked him, although he probably would not have spoken about it," she added. *(Photographs courtesy of Candace Stockton.)*

Clarence Schubert – Brazito and Osage Bluff

The preparations made by Mary Messer to discuss her late father's military service became a family affair, highlighted by photographs and other military mementos strewn across tables in her home near Russellville. Her father, a veteran of World War II, was not one to speak of his military service and the mementos left behind have become clues for his family members seeking to learn more about the role he played in the war.

"My father, Clarence Schubert, was born in 1914 and was raised with his five siblings on a farm near Brazito," Messer explained. "While growing up, he was a member of St. John's Lutheran Church in Stringtown and attended the parish school there through the eighth grade," she added.

Schubert was married with four children when he was inducted into the U.S. Army in 1944. During World War II, he served with an engineer battalion that built roads in Europe under combat conditions. Courtesy of Mary Messer

Upon finishing his formal education at Stringtown, Schubert worked on his father's farm for a few years before becoming involved in the construction trades. For the next several years, he was employed by local contractors and gained experience as a carpenter.

On July 10, 1937, Schubert married Marie Jacobs—a native of Osage Bluffs—at St. Paul's Lutheran Church in California. The couple became parents to four children before World War II, which soon brought unanticipated changes to their married life.

"During the early part of the war, my father still worked as a carpenter for contractors that built barracks and other structures at Camp Crowder (Neosho, Missouri) and at Ft. Leonard Wood," Messer said. "But his discharge documents show that he went to Jefferson Barracks in February 1944 for a physical and was classified as physically fit."

Private Clarence Schubert was inducted into the U.S. Army at Jefferson Barracks on March 29, 1944, and then boarded a train destined for Camp Bowie, Texas. Following his arrival, he became a member of Company A, 1264th Engineer Combat Battalion and embarked upon a regimen of training in preparation for the war in Europe. The first few weeks of their initial training included calisthenics, close-order drills, marksmanship, map reading, and road marches. Next came their introduction to subjects tailored to prepare them for the engineering work they would likely perform overseas— demolitions, concealment of mines, reconnaissance, and building fixed and floating bridges.

Schubert was promoted to private first class in early August 1944 and received a fifteen-day furlough the following month, returning to his family in Mid-Missouri. Then, it was back to Camp Bowie, where he joined his fellow soldiers in prepping their equipment for deployment.

"Late on the afternoon of October 11, the battalion was given the order to move and was marched with full field packs, rifles, and steel helmets to a nearby field," explained *The History of the 1264th Engineer Combat Battalion*. The book further noted that ". . . at 9:00 p.m. the men loaded up in trucks and headed for the station. As the train left the station platform, the band struck up 'Auld Lang Syne.' The men felt a touch of nostalgia steal over them as the train left Texas."

The rail journey eventually carried them to Camp Kilmer, New Jersey, where they soon boarded a troop ship that departed the U.S. on October 22, 1944. Arriving at a port near Somerset, England less than two weeks later, their battalion headquarters were established, and unit training continued. Military records indicate they began the next step of their journey on Christmas Day, boarding a ship that transported them across the English Channel to Cherbourg, France.

"Cherbourg was in shambles, a broken city," the battalion history explained. "Late in the afternoon, in lowering twilight, we 'hit the beach,' setting our feet on French soil."

The next six months were defined as a "nomadic movement," as the battalion followed the war across Belgium, the Netherlands, and into Germany. Schubert and soldiers of the battalion not only fought bitter cold temperatures but worked to build roads under combat conditions. Oftentimes, the roads were constructed using heavy logs covered with a wire mesh buried under fourteen inches of gravel and rock. In March 1945, the battalion supported the Rhine crossing by delivering floating bridge components and provided area security while under enemy shelling and gunfire.

The war in Europe came to an end in early May 1945, but Schubert and the battalion remained in Germany for the next several months as part of the occupational forces. Spending much of their time in the historic German town of Eisenach, he preserved his experiences through stacks of photographs featuring sites he visited in addition to a recreational trip to Paris.

Schubert's discharge documents denote his return to the states on October 24, 1945. His separation from the U.S. Army occurred five days later at Jefferson Barracks, having achieved the rank of Technician Fourth Grade.

"After my father came home, he somehow got the name of 'Speed Schubert' and moved the family to a house on a farm near Osage Bend," said Mary Messer. "I was born a few years later and my father continued his work as a carpenter, spending many years with the Roy Scheperle Construction Company and Paul R. Prost Construction." She continued, "My parents later built a house on Route E and my father worked as a union carpenter for more than fifty years."

The veteran later joined the American Legion but chose to keep any memories and stories of his military experiences to himself. He was eighty-five years old when he passed away in 1999 and now lies at rest alongside his wife in the cemetery of Immanuel Lutheran Church in Honey Creek.

"In his later years, at holiday gatherings and other activities, he might share a little bit about some trinket he had brought home from the war but didn't talk about combat or the work they did over there," said his grandson, Mark Messer.

Sorting through stacks of vintage photographs, military medals, and assorted foreign military uniform items Schubert brought back from the war, Mary Messer added, "This is all part of his memory and something that we as a family enjoy looking through to get to know him a little better." *(Photographs courtesy of Mary Messer.)*

CHAPTER 2

Agriculture

The Miller – Atkinson Farm – Near Mt. Pleasant

In December 1965, Curt and DeeEllen Atkinson purchased a farm located four and a half miles northeast of Eldon that possesses a fascinating history for both their family and Miller County. The property, which now contains only 252 acres of the original 640 acres, was established in 1838 by Curt Atkinson's great-great-great-grandfather, William Miller, who was an early area pioneer and responsible for the naming of the county.

A native of West Virginia, William Miller married Sarah Mulkey in Cooper County in 1820. In the book "Judge Jenkins' History of Miller County," it was written, "On May 2, 1837, the first session of the County Court was held in the log house of William Miller by the Osage River, near the mouth of the Saline Creek."

DeeEllen Atkinson explained, "In 1837, William Miller delivered a petition signed by area residents to the capitol in Jefferson City asking that the new county being formed be given the name 'Miller' for the ex-governor, John Miller."

Historical records provided by Atkinson note the county was supposed to have been named for Pinckney Story Miller, a son of William's and reputedly the first white male child born in the area. However, William did not believe the state legislature would agree to name a county for the son of a local farmer, which is why he requested—and succeeded—in having it named for a former governor.

Several years ago, this photograph was found in the attic of a house near the Miller-Atkinson Farm. It features John Mulkey Tate Miller standing in front of the home he built in 1884.

William Miller established his new farm on January 6, 1838, on what is now Kent Road, a gravel thoroughfare that stretches between U.S. Highway 54 and Highway FF west of Mt. Pleasant. Gwen Gunn

Shoemaker and Grace Adams Farmer explained in a book about the Miller family published in 1971 that the original 640 acres owned by William Miller were ultimately cut into smaller sections.

"Later, William moved near Mt. Pleasant where he bought a tract of cleared land and entered more," wrote Shoemaker and Farmer. "He gave each of his children 100 acres when they married, or its equivalent."

On February 8, 1838, a month after Willam established his farm near Mt. Pleasant, he and his wife welcomed a son, John Mulkey Tate Miller. At the time of John's birth, William and his wife were already parents to eight children and would go on to raise a total of twelve.

In an article appearing in the *Eldon Advertiser* on February 19, 1987, Miller County historian Peggy Smith Hake explained that William Miller remained involved in political affairs and the construction of roads in townships within the county.

She wrote, ". . . the first election judge for Osage Township in July 1837 was William Miller; William Miller and Thomas Sorter were overseers of the Tuscumbia-California Road constructed through Saline Township in 1837; in 1841, William Miller was appointed by Missouri's General Assembly as a road commissioner of the Tuscumbia-Springfield Road . . ."

William's son, John Mulkey Tate Miller, helped carry forth his father's agricultural legacy by assuming the responsibilities as a farmer. He built a house on the property in 1884 that is still being used to this day.

According to the *Eldon Advertiser* on June 6, 1918, John Miller was known as "Uncle Jack" to his close acquaintances. Additionally, he "became a charter member of the church at Mt. Pleasant where he served as Elder until 1908 when he removed his membership to the Christian church at Olean ..."

Years later, John Miller's son, George, continued the family legacy as a farmer and, like his father, was an active member of Mt.

Pleasant Church. Sadly, the seventy-three-year-old was killed in 1944 after his car was struck by a Rock Island locomotive while crossing the railroad tracks east of Mt. Pleasant.

"My late husband and I, Curt Atkinson, purchased the farm in 1965," said DeeEllen Atkinson. "It had been owned by his great uncle and aunt, Ralph and Josephine Atkinson," she added.

DeeEllen and her husband made several renovations and additions to the house built by John Mulkey Tate Miller in 1884. They had been informed by William "Ernest" Miller— a nephew of John Mulkey Tate Miller—that a cornerstone had been laid under the front hallway of the house and situated so that each room was in a different section of the 640 acres owned by William Miller.

"There had been no running water in the house since Aunt Josephine didn't want a hole cut in the house to supply water," said DeeEllen. "Shortly after we bought the property, a bathroom was put in, as well as a kitchen update, with running water." She continued, "Several years ago, we had to make a repair to the floor and sure enough we found the chiseled cornerstone marker that verified what we had been told by Ernest Miller."

In 2013, the farm and property earned the designation of a "Missouri Century Farm." There have been many changes made to the 1884 home and none of the original barns and outbuildings exist on the farm, yet the story of the Miller family remains etched in local history.

Atkinson explained, "The property has many interesting stories to share—some of which may never be known. But the house and land help preserve the story of the Miller family and highlights the important role they played in both the organization and settlement of Miller County and the surrounding areas." (*Photographs courtesy of DeeEllen Atkinson.*)

The Emil Farris Farm – South of Russellville

When Jamie Sullivan and her husband were looking at purchasing a farm in 2016 located several miles south of Russellville, she asked her grandfather to share his opinion of the property. She then discovered that it was the same farm where her grandfather had been raised decades earlier and, in addition to once being the site of illegal moonshine production, it had been lost by her family during the financially distressing period of the Great Depression.

"My husband and I purchased the property and there is still the old barn and house on the property," Sullivan shared. "We lived in the old house until we were able to build a new home," she added.

Her grandfather, the late Oliver "Vernon" Farris shared stories about growing up on the farm, explaining that his father, Emil Farris, would use a team of horses to plant corn along the Moreau and later harvest it by hand. Raised a short distance to the west, Emil Farris purchased the farm in the early 1930s when it was auctioned on the

Cole County Courthouse steps after the death of Wilson Spencer Webb, a wealthy land investor from Kansas City.

The father of three sons, Emil was known by locals to have engaged in bootlegging during Prohibition. In an attempt to conceal his activities from the revenue agent he cooked his moonshine in one of the two caves on the property, the larger of which was called "Buzzard Cave."

"One of the family stories that has been handed down is that after Emil made his moonshine in the cave, he would then sell it out of the barn on the property," Sullivan said. "The person wishing to make a purchase had to have a special knock in order to enter." She further explained, "Apparently one guy just walked into the barn and didn't knock, and my great-grandfather was holding an axe, ready to strike him." Pausing she added, "But … apparently everything worked out."

Emil Farris, standing, is pictured with his wife, Ethel and three sons, from left: John, Vernon and Virgle. Emil and his family lived on a farm seven miles south of Russellville that they lost in the early 1940s. In 2016, the farm returned to the Farris family when purchased by his great-granddaughter and her husband.

According to family lore, Emil received word that a revenue agent had caught wind of the illegal moonshine production he was conducting and was preparing to conduct a raid. To prevent being caught, he fed all the corn mash to his pigs, which then became drunk and ran off across the river.

"It took him some time to find all of those drunk pigs," Sullivan chuckled.

Emil's older brother, Raymond, was also reputed to have engaged in the illegal production of spirits during Prohibition at his residence in the Brazito area. When revenue agents raided his property, he was arrested after being found hiding under a chicken coop.

On a farm adjoining the Farris's lived a Black family comprised of several siblings, the elder of whom was Charles Elmer Tyree. Known to locals as "Punkin" Tyree, he was mechanically inclined and often employed by Emil Farris to make repairs on his farm equipment.

"Punkin would often be at the house to do work for my great-grandfather," she said. "My great-grandmother would always offer him something to eat, but for some reason, he refused to eat in the house and instead went outside to eat on the porch." She added, "He was a very nice man that was well respected by all the neighbors, I have been told."

Emil and his wife, Ethel Blank, raised three sons. Vernon, who was the youngest and born in 1930, told his granddaughter that while he was growing up, their family was the only one in the area that owned a radio.

"He said that he was an eleven-year-old boy when he and his family were listening to the radio and heard that the Japanese had bombed Pearl Harbor," Sullivan said. "His parents then told him to run and tell all of the neighbors that war was coming."

The farm, in addition to being used to raise crops and livestock, had an old spring that was used by both Emil and his neighbors to water horses. Sadly, in the early 1940s, the lingering financial challenges of the Great Depression resulted in him losing the farm on which he had diligently toiled for over a decade.

For the remainder of his working life, Emil Farris never again owned a farm. Instead, he lived on a farm he rented near Russellville. The eighty-one-year-old retired farmer passed away in 1978 and was laid to rest in Enloe Cemetery near Russellville; his wife, Ethel, died in 1996. In the decades after losing the farm, it underwent several changes in ownership. As Sullivan explained, it was a fortuitous moment when she and her husband discovered that the farm they had purchased was once owned by her great-grandfather.

"My grandfather excitedly recalled spending some of his early years on the farm with us," Sullivan said. "He passed away in 2020 but it was so special to have him come over and show us things like where an old road once passed through the property and tell us stories like the bootlegging that occurred here." She continued, "It has been so important to learn the history of this place and know that it has returned to the Farris family. Having these stories shared helps make sure that I can preserve its legacy for my children and grandchildren." *(Photographs courtesy of Jamie Sullivan.)*

The Henry Beck Farm – Honey Creek area

John Christopher Hedler, a native of Bayern, Germany, contributed to the agricultural foundation of the Midwest when immigrating to Missouri and purchasing his first expanse of farmland in a deed dated April 15, 1857, and signed by President Buchanan. This property was later acquired by the Beck family, with whom it has remained for several generations. Much of Hedler's life in Cole County was defined by hardship since he not only toiled to build a productive farm near Honey Creek but had to bury two stillborn daughters. In 1897, when his wife Katherina died, she was buried on the farm next to her daughters and Hedler moved to Jefferson City.

The *Westliche Post*, a German-language newspaper from St. Louis, noted that the ninety-year-old Hedler died because of serious injuries sustained from falling down a flight of stairs while sleepwalking on August 1, 1910. A Union Army veteran of the Civil War, he was laid to rest in the Jefferson City National Cemetery.

Hermetta Beck painted in 1973 this watercolor of the original house built by John Hedler around the Civil War. Originally a log cabin later covered with wood siding, the home is no longer inhabitable.

"My great-grandfather, Henry Beck, bought the farm from John Hedler some years before his death but we are not certain when the actual sale occurred," said Garry Beck. "Similar to many family farms during that timeframe, they engaged in a lot of agricultural activities like raising livestock, row cropping, and taking commodities like eggs and cream to sell in town."

The son of German immigrants, Henry Beck was born In Cole County in 1857 and was a lifelong member of Immanuel Lutheran Church in Honey Creek. In 1883, he married Leona Duenkel and the couple raised five children, including Rilius, a son born in 1890.

"Rilius was my grandfather and he helped my great-grandfather on the farm for many years," said Garry Beck. "He married Alvina Sommerer in 1916 and they had four children—Edna, Melinda, Edmund, who (sic) they called 'Buddy,' and my father, Herman." Beck continued, "In 1917, Rilius purchased the farm from his father. In addition to the normal farming operations, he established a couple of apple orchards and had a press he used to make cider. Rilius' father died in 1933 and his mother in 1952, and they are both buried at Immanuel Lutheran Church Cemetery."

While growing up, Garry Beck had the privilege of helping his grandfather around the farm and also listening as he shared mirthful stories about his youth, such as the way he learned to swim.

"When Rilius was a kid, he couldn't swim so a farmhand picked him up and threw him into a pond on the property," Garry Beck recalled. "My grandfather would always chuckle when he told me that story."

Rilius' first wife, Alvina, died in 1926 and he later married Helen Mueller, with whom he had no children.

During the Great Depression, Beck explained, Rilius briefly rented out the farm and went to work shoveling coal at the power plant once located west of the Capitol building in Jefferson City. He was later hired as a tower guard at the Missouri State Penitentiary.

"From what I was told by family, he was part of a burial detail for a Black inmate that died and was to be quietly buried at the penitentiary," Beck said. "Apparently, the man's family came down from either Kansas City or St. Louis and my grandfather officiated the funeral because he felt that it needed to be done."

Family lore notes that his grandfather eventually left his job as a tower guard because even though he was a crack shot with a rifle, he had no desire to ever shoot an escaping inmate. Returning to his farm, Rilius supplemented his farm work by hunting raccoons and other small game, often traveling to Jefferson City to sell the meat. His children helped him around the farm until World War II began to unfold.

"My father, Herman, was the oldest and was drafted into the U.S. Army," Beck said. "He ended up serving as an infantry soldier in the Pacific and participated in the Battle of Leyte Gulf. In the Philippines, he was wounded and received a Purple Heart."

In the years following his wartime service, Herman married Barbara Miller. They became parents to both Garry and his sister, Hermetta. Herman worked for many years in Jefferson City, eventually retiring from Schriefer's Office Machines and Equipment. In his free time, he came to help his brother, Buddy, and their father on the farm.

Rilius passed away in 1980 followed by his second wife, Helen, in 1994; the couple was buried at the Lutheran church in Honey Creek. Buddy took over the lion's share of the farm duties and, until the early 1980s, lived in the log cabin built more than a century earlier by the farm's original owner, John Hedler. Garry Beck's father, Herman, died in 1999 and his Uncle Buddy passed away in 2007. He and his sister inherited part of the farm from their father and were able to purchase the remaining property. The siblings are now the fourth generation of Becks to own the 178-acre farm, which proudly bears the designation as a Missouri Century Farm.

"Up into the 1960s it was common to see farms of this size in this area that had been owned by a particular family for generations," said Garry Beck. "But it is becoming less common since many of these farms are being sold off so that subdivisions and similar things can be built." He added, "My sister and I are the heirs of this Beck legacy and we have no children that we can pass it to, so it may end with us. Times change, but we want to ensure that the story of this farm and those who worked to build it are remembered." *(Photographs courtesy of Garry Beck.)*

The Judge Henry Smith Farm – Henley

In recent years, Kim Smith has explored an interest in learning the history of his farm near Henley and the family member who established it in the 1870s. His research has revealed an intriguing story about a man raised in a pioneering Cole County family, who, despite having only a limited educational foundation, was elected presiding judge of the Cole County court system.

"My great-great-grandfather was Henry Marion Smith, born on June 23, 1848, on his parents' farm near Hickory Hill," explained Kim Smith. "He was only ten years old when his father died but he was educated in the local one-room schools and later taught in some of these schools," he added.

Smith married Mary Jane Reavis, a resident of the Henley area, on January 16, 1870, and being energetic in his endeavors, purchased his first farm three miles east of his mother's home several months later. This farm he sold seven years later and it was then he purchased a new farm near Henley, which remains in the family to this day.

"He raised cattle and became a successful stock dealer," Kim Smith explained. "On the property, he built a two-story log cabin and that's where he raised three sons and two daughters."

Pictured is the two-story log cabin built as a home in the 1870s by Judge Henry Smith. The historic structure fell victim to arson several years ago.

A person of devoted faith, the March 30, 1933 edition of the *Jefferson City Post-Tribune*, noted that Smith became "one of the organizers of and charter members of the Hickory Hill Baptist Church." It was here that he also served as a deacon and often found enjoyment serving as a song leader.

Not one to remain idle, Smith was a member of the Democratic party, the ticket on which he was elected as presiding judge for the Cole County court on

November 8, 1878. Several years later, in 1886, he was elected a district judge and held this seat for one term.

"What is very interesting is that he also served as a justice of the peace for the Clark Township and helped oversee the construction and maintenance of the roads in the area," said Kim Smith. "All of this was done while he was working as a judge and maintaining the stock operations on his farm."

The judge's farm also possesses an interesting connection to local Civil War-era lore. On the property, there is a cave that is often referred to as "Crabtree Cave," where a guerrilla general by the name of Crabtree used it as one of his hiding places after attacking Union troops and northern sympathizers.

"There seem to be some conflicting stories that have been told about Crabtree," Kim Smith said. "One of the documents I have noted that Crabtree was shot in a nearby barn and that he either crawled to the cave or was helped there by his men. Regardless," he added, "he supposedly was found dead there." He continued, "Apparently after being found, he was loaded on a wagon by my great-great-grandfather and a couple of local men and then buried near the Old Teal Bottom Schoolhouse. Some histories state that his body was later exhumed and moved to another location, though no one seems to be certain where his grave actually is since it was likely unmarked."

Despite the legend surrounding this event, Judge Smith's name remained a respected part of Henley area happenings. As the years passed, one of his sons, James Kearney Smith, helped out on the farm while pursuing a path marginally similar to his father's.

"James Kearney was my great-grandfather and he spent a lot of time on horseback and out-of-state," said Kim Smith. "He participated in a lot of cattle drives and ran the stockyards in Henley for the last fifteen years of this life."

The eighty-four-year-old Judge Smith passed away in March 1933; his widow died three years later. They are both interred in Hickory Hill Cemetery near the church where they had been members for decades. The farm, which was approximately 400 acres in size, was split between two of his sons still living in the area. It has since passed through the family and is now owned by Kim Smith.

In 1937, four years after Judge Smith's death, the *Miller-County Autogram* noted that Clem Schmitz was working near an old building on the late judge's farm when he found a one-half-cent U.S. coin dating to 1835. The building near which it was found was at the time being used as a workshop but had once served as a courtroom for Judge Smith.

"Judge Smith's log cabin was covered with siding in later years and I once hoped to get it on some form of historic register," said Kim Smith. "However, several years ago, there were some arsonists going around torching old barns and houses." Pausing, he added, "And the judge's house was the last one they burned."

Many years ago, as Kim Smith was walking through the Cole County Courthouse, he glanced up at a painting that hung on the wall, realizing the image was of his great-great-grandfather.

"Those who serve in law enforcement and legal professions have always been held in high esteem in my family and it was a proud moment to see that picture of my great-great-grandfather in the courthouse." He added, "And that was only part of his story, if you also consider his work as a stock dealer, running a farm and being active in the church. These are the types of people who helped build Cole County and we can still learn from their selfless example." (*Photographs courtesy of Kim Smith.*)

The Julius Engelbrecht Farm – Ambrose Community (Brazito)

The Engelbrecht Farm on Tanner Bridge Road near Brazito is an example of a Missouri family farm that represents the dedicated spirit of families who learned to work together for survival. Many of these farms, though not creating substantial wealth and fame for the owners, have oftentimes provided a lifeline through difficult times such as the Great Depression.

Martin J. Engelbrecht, the son of German immigrants, married Katherine Duenckel in 1885, and the couple eventually settled in the Brazito community. Having refined skills in working with metal, he soon opened a blacksmith shop and acquired the income to purchase a farm.

"John Grethlein sold the farm to Martin Engelbrecht in 1897 for $1,950," said Michael Engelbrecht, when discussing his great-grandfather. "The farm was 145 acres and there was already a house on the property, but Martin and his wife didn't live there; they built a beautiful four-story house a short distance to the west," he added. He continued, "The farm has had several nicknames like 'Engelbrecht's Everglades' because there is rich soil and a bunch of springs. There is also a tributary of the original Honey Creek (for which the nearby community is named) that runs through the middle of the property."

Julius Engelbrecht is pictured in his wedding photograph from 1917 when he married Barbara Sommerer. The legacy of the Engelbrecht farm near Brazito dates back to 1897, when his father, Martin Engelbrecht, purchased the 145-acre property.

Julius, the older of Martin's two sons, married Barbara Sommerer in 1916. Having grown rather affluent through this blacksmithing work, Martin sold the farm to Julius on February 1, 1917, for $2,500.

Michael Engelbrecht explained, "The house that was on the farm when my great-grandfather Martin purchased the place was too small to raise a family. Julius ordered house plans from Montgomery Ward and they cut timber on the place to build a bigger home, which is the one now on the property."

The old barn is now gone although several outbuildings with limestone foundations remain. Throughout the years, the farm has been used to grow hay for horses and later evolved into row cropping, a location to raise cattle and poultry, and a dairy farm in addition to a large peach orchard.

Martin Engelbrecht, pictured, and his brother Leroy took over the farm from their father, Julius. He is pictured with his wife, Patricia.

The Engelbrecht family were members of Immanuel Lutheran Church at nearby Honey Creek and became actively involved in efforts to share their love of agriculture with youth in the surrounding area.

"The Ambrose 4-H Club derives its name from Ambrose School where the 4-H Club had its first meeting in 1936," noted the *Sunday News and Tribune* on October 4, 1970. "There were 20 members in the original organization with Julius Engelbrecht and Miss Rosalyn Sappenfield as leaders."

The agricultural influence Julius Engelbrecht had on the local youth through his dedication to the Ambrose 4-H Club has had a lasting impact. The late Ralph Popp, a member of the club in its early days, went on to establish Popp's Lawn and Garden. Additionally, the Trinklein family, many of whom were involved in the 4-H, remains a name associated with a well-known local greenhouse business.

Julius's six children—Alma, Helen, Martin, Mary Ann, Alice, and Leroy—all participated in 4-H. They were able to support the family farm through various projects by raising baby chicks, canning assorted foods, and repairing fences. These were all skills that helped ensure the farm survived in the coming years.

"I was told that ours was the first farm in Cole County to be terraced through a cooperative project with the University of Missouri," Michael Engelbrecht said. "Also, they planted multi-flora roses in the fencerows to create a hedge back before they were considered an invasive species of plant," he added.

Michael Engelbrecht shared that his father, Martin, although being rather small in stature because of infant polio, experienced a growth spurt and was able to enlist in the Missouri National Guard. After serving in the Korean War, he earned his agricultural engineering degree from the University of Missouri.

"My father and his brother, Leroy, became partners in the farm in 1955," said Engelbrecht. "Then, my father became an extension agent for the University of Missouri in southern Missouri and married my mother in 1958. I was born in 1959, and the following year my father moved back to the farm because Julius was having trouble keeping it up because of his age."

Eventually, Martin Engelbrecht became the Farm Bureau agent for the county and was able to help pay off the farm debts. He and Leroy then set aside ten acres where each of their families would live; Martin's section included the home built in 1917 by their father, and Leroy built a home on the opposite side of the farm. The remaining 125 acres were co-owned and farmed by both brothers.

Changes and updates have been occurring throughout the decades with electricity coming to the farm in 1947 and the Engelbrecht farmhouse receiving indoor plumbing in 1960. Martin and Leroy have both passed away but their widows continue to live on their respective ten-acre properties. The families of Leroy and Martin continue to share the responsibility of caring for the remaining 125 acres.

Glancing down Tanner Bridge Road, Michael Engelbrecht explained that there were some family farms in the area that no longer exist because they have been sold and developed into residential properties. However, the Engelbrecht Farm has weathered economic difficulties and continues to represent a shared family legacy.

"Here on this farm, we are living the history of not only the Engelbrecht family but many others in the community," he said. "This farm became a lifeline for our family during the Great Depression and although it's not made anyone rich, it has helped many survive. And part of that survival is the connections we made to other families in the area. By trading goods, and services and working together, many families around here were able to move forward. Those necessary connections among neighbors are often a part of history that gets lost in the telling." *(Photographs courtesy of Michael Engelbrecht.)*

The Roark-Templeton-Gordon Farm – Southwest of Russellville

Situated along West Brazito Road seven miles southwest of Russellville is a hilly and tree-covered expanse of property known as the Roark-Templeton-Gordon Farm. It has earned the nickname "Rocky Top Farm" by Ron Gordon because of its terrain and now entering it's sixth-generation of family ownership. Like many Missouri Century Farms, it survives as a fascinating example of both local family and agricultural history.

Moses Campbell Roark, a native of Kentucky, settled in Cole County with his wife, Matilda Howard. The couple, prior to moving to Benton County, Missouri, raised three sons. The youngest of their sons, John Jacob Roark, later established the roots of the family-owned farm.

"J.J. (John Jacob) Roark purchased forty acres in 1887, an additional twenty acres in 1893, and finally sixteen acres in 1910," said Ron Gordon. "J.J. married Sarah Arney and then her sister, Frances Arney, married my great-grandfather, Clark Templeton." He added, "J.J. ended up being referred to as 'Uncle John Roark' in our family."

Although the seventy-six-acre property was never owned by Clark Templeton, his son, Richard (Fred) Templeton, along with his

The Roark-Templeton-Gordon Farm along West Brazito Road in southern Cole County became a Missouri Century Farm in 2020, but was established in 1887. Pictured are the fifth-generation owners, Ron and Linda Gordon. Courtesy of Jeremy P. Amick

wife, Christena (Tena), farmed the property while helping to care for an aged J.J. Roark after his wife died in 1924.

"Because of all that my grandparents, Fred and Tena, had done to take care of him in his advanced years, J.J. Roark basically gave them the seventy-six acres for one dollar back in 1932," said Ron Gordon.

Later the same year, J.J. Roark passed away and was laid to rest in Matheis Cemetery near Enon, alongside his beloved wife. Years later, Arthur Gordon married Helen, a daughter of Fred and Tena Templeton. Sadly, in 1940, Helen passed away when only twenty years old after giving birth to a son, Ron.

"After my mother died, my father couldn't find work around here so he moved to Kansas City and went to work for Safeway," said Ron Gordon. "I lived on the farm and was raised by my grandparents—Fred and Tena Templeton." In a heartfelt tribute, he added, "My grandmother never got over losing my mother, but she was a wonderful woman who loved me deeply." He continued, "I can remember helping my grandfather farm with horses. Eventually, I sold two cows and purchased the first tractor for the farm, a Farmall F-12. Back then, we grew corn, oats, and wheat, raised cattle and sold Grade C milk by milking seven or eight cows," he added.

The family lived in a small house on the farm that had been expanded around a log cabin that was likely built by the initial farm owner, J.J. Roark. A county road once passed in front of the house, but was condemned several decades ago and is now indiscernible because of undergrowth.

Arthur Gordon, though continuing to live in the Kansas City area, purchased an adjoining seventy-four-acre farm in 1945 for $1,800. Nine years later, he purchased the seventy-six-acre farm from his father-in-law, Fred Templeton, for $4,000 and combined the two into a 150-acre farm.

Ron Gordon said, "Fred and Tena Templeton took the money my father paid them for the farm and purchased a home on Smith Street in Russellville. I lived with them there for several years while my father rented the farm to his brother, Earmen."

After graduating from Russellville High School in 1958, Ron Gordon married Linda Wagner from Centertown in 1960. His grandmother, Tena, passed away in 1961 and her husband died in 1970. Gordon was able to purchase his grandparents' home in Russellville, where he and his wife for many years raised their two daughters.

In 1972, Ron Gordon moved his family to the farm, first living in a mobile home since the original homestead where he had been raised was no longer habitable. Four years later, he built a log cabin on the property and that is where he and his wife continue to reside. The original log home has been covered in metal siding and is now used for storage. These days, the farm is no longer cultivated in crops, but hay is still cut on the property. Also, Ron has been active in a local tractor club and has restored many of these historic farm implements including a Farmall F-12 similar to the first tractor he purchased in his youth.

The years have witnessed the removal of barns and other structures on the property along with additions such as a small lake and a cabin. But as Gordon explained, the picturesque landscape that has produced many good memories is being passed on to his children, ensuring the farm remains in the family as it enters its sixth generation of ownership.

"This farm is the story of a lot of hard-working people who toiled to make a living and a better life for others in our family," said Gordon. "There were a lot of people who intermingled over the years and had to be in the right place at the right time to make everything work." Pausing in reflection, he added, "I've seen some changes, like going from horses to tractors and then getting electricity in 1948. The stories that are involved in our farm—and other local farms— created the backbone of agriculture in this area and our family is privileged to have been a part of it all." *(Photographs courtesy of Jeremy P. Ämick.)*

Lorenz Strobel–– *Lohman*

Food production became a critical component of the United States' success during World War II. Yet there were many farm families that not only struggled to produce the staples necessary on both the home front and in overseas combat zones but frequently did so without the assistance of children who had been drafted to serve in the Armed Forces.

Lorenz Strobel fell into such circumstances during his youth.

Born in 1924 and growing up on his family's farm northwest of Lohman, he was the fourth oldest in a family of three boys and three girls. In addition to the hard days engaged in farm work, he attended the nearby St. Paul's Lutheran Church with his family, becoming a confirmed member in 1939.

"He attended the old Lohman School, which is now being used as the Community Center," said his wife, Ellen Strobel. "Since it didn't have high school classes, he and several others from the area traveled to the high school in Jefferson City." She continued, "But after two years, he quit school so that he could stay home to help his parents on the farm."

While involved in his agricultural work, Strobel, like many others, was reading the newspapers and listening to conversations in the community regarding the U.S. entering World War II following the attack on Pearl Harbor. Soon, his older brother, Oscar, left home after he was drafted into the U.S. Army in December 1942.

"Lorenz and I had met in the community, mostly through church, and then began dating," said Ellen Strobel. "But

Strobel completed his basic training at Fort Hood, Texas, and was later assigned to Company A, 47th Engineers.

then he received his draft notice and left for the Army in February 1945."

This left only one brother, seven-year-old Hugo, along with three sisters, to help their parents keep the farm afloat. Fortunately, in December 1945, his older brother Oscar was released from the Army after serving in the Marshall Islands with a signal company and returned to the Lohman area.

Following his induction at Jefferson Barracks, Lorenz Strobel was sent to Fort Hood, Texas, for several weeks of basic combat training. This was followed by six weeks of engineering school during which he was instructed on the operation of different tractors and bulldozers.

Assigned to Company A, 47th Engineers Construction Battalion, Strobel was first deployed to the Philippines, departing the U.S. aboard a troop ship on September 9, 1945, seven days after the surrender of Japan.

"There wasn't a lot that he said about his service, but he did talk about building roads in the Philippines," his wife recalled. "He mentioned about being in a hurricane while he was there and having to seek cover in some buildings that ended up being damaged."

Discharge records indicate Strobel served as a construction foreman with the engineering company and later transferred to Okinawa. It was here that the 47th Engineers were engaged in a number of projects including the construction of Quonset huts that were used as housing. In October 1946, he left Okinawa and sailed back to the United States. He was eventually sent to Fort Sheridan, Illinois, where he received his discharge as a staff sergeant on December 9, 1946.

"Whenever he came home from the service, he worked a couple of years with his brother-in-law building houses," said Ellen Strobel. "And in 1948, we were married at St. Paul's Lutheran Church in Lohman."

The couple went on to raise two sons and a daughter but sadly lost one child at only five years of age.

Strobel quickly returned to his pre-service focus by assisting his father on their farm. When his father passed away in 1951, Strobel took over the farm and later operated it in partnership with his brother, Hugo, who was the youngest son of the family. Hugo was drafted into the Army in 1958 and served two years in Germany with an Ordnance Company.

Lorenz Strobel's military service became but a footnote in his greater legacy as he continued to embrace public service that included fifty years on the board of Farmer's Bank of Lohman, many of which were spent as board president. Additionally, he was a member of the board of his local MFA. He volunteered as a leader of the 4-H board, and the Cole County Extension Council and actively participated in a number of offices within St. Paul's Lutheran Church, such as several decades as the Sunday school superintendent. For many years, he and his wife placed flags on the graves of veterans buried in their church cemetery.

"One thing that he really enjoyed was being able to go fishing," said his wife, Ellen, in mirthful reflection. "He would come home from church on Sunday and want to have lunch as quickly as possible so that he could get back outdoors." She continued, "He also enjoyed cooking molasses with several of the Heidbreder brothers."

On March 11, 2014, the eighty-nine-year-old veteran passed away. He was laid to rest with full military honors in the cemetery of St. Paul's Lutheran Church. A long-time member of both the American Legion and Veterans of Foreign Wars, Ellen Strobel noted that prior to his passing, her husband truly enjoyed his visit to the nation's military memorials as part of the Central Missouri Honor Flight.

She explained, "He didn't say much about his service but was very patriotic and enjoyed being around other veterans. I know that he thought a lot of his country and would always take things as they came while letting God take care of the rest." *(Photographs courtesy of Ellen Strobel.)*

CHAPTER 3

Education

Honey School – Stringtown

Partially hidden in a wooded area behind a house on Stringtown Station Road is a log cabin that was once the Honey School. (Some locals have referred to it as "Hiney School.") This rustic school sets on property once known as the Honey Farm. James Honey, an Irish immigrant, owned a significant amount of property in the area. In 1850, he donated a piece of property on a hill near the eastern terminus of Hemstreet Road for the building of the former St. Joseph Catholic Mission. This mission church held its last mass in 1894 and the property and adjacent cemetery are now cared for by St. Michael Catholic Church in Russellville.

Though records are sparse on the matter, it is believed that Honey School was built after the Civil War, becoming the first in the Stringtown and Lohman areas. According to a public sale bill from 1968, an old walnut schoolmaster desk from 1870, which had been removed from Honey School, was sold at auction.

In reflections penned by Oswald W. Soell prior to his death in 1972, he explained that the "school had one door and two windows and was used until 1908." Soell also noted that the school was later sold to Adam Erhart and eventually owned by his son-in-law, Jewell Scott.

In 1909, a year after the log school was closed, a gravel/concrete schoolhouse was built approximately a mile to the west on Stringtown Station Road. Known

This photograph was taken of students at Honey School on January 15, 1896. First row, left to right: Bessie Thompson, Hilda Linsenbardt, Rosetta Weber Schneider, Tracie Huettenmeyer and Augusta Linsenbardt Kirchner. Second row: Christen Pistel, Arthur Thompson, Bell Kautsch, Bill Linsenbardt, William Huettenmeyer, Otto Kiesling and John Kiesling. Third row: First student unidentified, second student unidentified, Minnie Thompson Vogel, Grace Umsted (teacher), Lula Thompson Strobel, fifth, sixth and seventh students unidentified. Courtesy of Mark Weber

as Stringtown School, this second schoolhouse no longer exists but was located behind the current home of Harry and Jana Thompson near the junction of Walnut Acres Road.

The Honey School has survived for more than a century and a half, yet not without revealing some of its wrinkles. Located on private property, the log schoolhouse will someday be reclaimed by the earth but thankfully a part of its glorious past has been preserved to share with future generations.

Zion Public School – Near the community of Zion

Situated near Zion Lutheran Church on a private drive of Zion Road, a small, white building stands as a testament to a bygone means of education—the one-room school district. Other area schoolhouses, such as the Corinth School and the Zion Parochial School, have long been demolished, deleting a connection to the past that continues to fade with the passing years.

"We are not sure when this school (Zion Public School) was first built," wrote the late Palmer Scheperle, an area historian who wrote the book *History of the Scheperle Family in America*. He added, "It is documented that Pastor (Carl) Thurow was teaching at the public school after 1868. Another source revealed that the first public school was originally located where the present Zion (Lutheran) Church now stands."

An article in the *State Republican* printed on January 28, 1892, helped verify the existence of the Zion Public School at that time. The paper reported, "The 'Spelling Match' given at the Zion school

John Nieghorn, who died in 1899, left property and money through his estate for the Zion Public School. Courtesy of Gary Schmutzler

Sunday eve., was well attended and also interesting by the participation therein of prominent ladies and gentlemen of this vicinity."

The history of the Zion Public School has been fogged by the passage of decades, evidenced by Scheplerle's writings that note the property for the current schoolhouse was located on land supposedly donated by Otto Nieghorn. However, descendants of the Nieghorn family possess documents that indicate otherwise.

A ledger related to the settlement of the estate of (Johann) John Nieghorn, who was the grandfather of Otto Nieghorn and died in 1899, was not fully settled until several years later. Through his estate, there was property and some money designated for a school.

Noel Fischer, the current owner of the property on which the school stands, explained, "The Nieghorn family offered three acres of land and $600 for the school to be built (the money came from the estate of John Nieghorn). The most recent schoolhouse was erected in 1903 and had an entryway that was used for hanging up coats and then students walked into a single, large classroom," he added.

Local resident Celia Elizabeth (Loesch) Stake, who was born in 1876, attended the Zion Public School prior to moving to Jefferson City with her family in the 1890s, where she was active in Trinity Lutheran Church.

Doris Schmutzler remarked, "My grandfather, Harry Ehrhardt, born in 1888, attended what he called 'the English school,' after graduating from the parochial school at Zion Lutheran Church, which was taught in German. His father, Nick, wanted him to continue his education because the Zion Public School taught advanced courses in the English language."

Records show that Miss Margaret George, whose family was from the Centertown area, resigned her teaching position at Zion Public School in the early weeks of 1929; she was replaced by Bonnie Spalding of the Eugene area.

The class size of one-room schools often varied, depending upon a recipe of factors such as the number of families living in the vicinity of the schoolhouse. A few weeks after Ms. Spalding took over the teaching responsibilities at Zion Public School, Ernest Loesch was the only student in the graduating class. By early 1935, Zion Public School had grown to the extent that it had a pool of students large enough to put on a play for the entertainment of the public that was titled "Cabbage or Dollars."

"Further Cole County organizations for the 1943 Red Cross War Fund Campaign have been perfected and meetings will be held this week and next in rural communities," the *Sunday News and Tribune* noted on March 14, 1943.

The meetings featured films and entertainment structured to create enthusiasm for the campaigns to raise funds in support of World

War II. One of these meetings was held at Zion Public School on March 7, 1943, and conducted under the leadership of Elder Jacobs. The following month, Elder Jacobs received commendation from the Red Cross after helping raise $517.90 for the war effort through his work in the Honey Creek, Brazito, and Zion neighborhoods.

Noel Fischer explained, "Zion Public School closed in the early 1940s and it was sold on a quit-claim deed to Eddie Loesch. For several years, Eddie used it as a hunting cabin and then he sold it to a fellow bricklayer, Mr. Humbrook." He continued, "Mr. Humbrook also used the building as a hunting lodge, dividing the large classroom into four smaller rooms and adding electricity. He then sold it to a Kennedy—a bachelor who lived there for several years."

Fischer further explained that his father, Norman, owned the property surrounding the schoolhouse, and when he did not see footprints outside the building after a snowstorm, went to check on Kennedy. Sadly, he discovered that he had passed away. Fischer's father purchased from Kennedy's relatives the schoolhouse and the three acres it sat upon. Years later, in the mid-1990s, Noel and his wife, Betty, purchased eighteen acres of Norman's property, which included the former Zion Public School.

"We still use it as a hunting lodge and I've taken care of it by repairing the chimney and keeping it painted every so often," Fischer said.

Though not possessing a deep connection to the schoolhouse since he and his family did not attend classes there, Fischer wishes to preserve this piece of disappearing local history so it can be remembered by the generations to come.

"The schoolhouse can't be seen from the highway and is on our private property, but it is important to us that it's taken care of and preserved," he said. "Someday, it will be neat to pass it on within our family so that it is a continued reminder of our local history." *(Primary photograph courtesy of Jeremy P. Amick.)*

Harmony Grove School – South of Jefferson City

The Loesch family was for many decades associated with the Corinth School near the Zion community south of Jefferson City. In the fall of 1946, when Candace (Loesch) Stockton was looking forward to beginning her elementary education at the same one-room schoolhouse her father had attended years earlier, she discovered that consolidation of school districts would require her to go to classes at Harmony Grove School in southwest Jefferson City. Located just south of the Jefferson City Country Club, the former Harmony Grove School came to be known not only as a building where local youth received their education but as a place where community groups could hold their meetings.

"The ladies of the Harmony School District met at the schoolhouse . . . and organized a club which will be known as the Inspiration Club," reported the *Daily Capital* News on January 5, 1923.

As the years passed, the schoolhouse would host gatherings for many community organizations such as the Harmony Extension Club, which became the first Women's Extension Club in Cole County when it was organized by T.F. Luker in 1930.

These community groups notwithstanding, the primary focus of activities within the small school building remained the education of area youth through the eighth grade. Despite its small size, Harmony Grove regularly earned both school district and individual teacher accolades for its dedication to educational efforts. Near the end of the school year in 1927, Harmony Grove's teacher, Marinda Rockelman, was presented with several gifts following the ceremonies during which five

Flora Bruning served as the teacher at Harmony Grove School in the early 1950s.

students graduated. Two years later, with Norma Jones serving as the teacher, the school graduated four students.

"I started at Harmony Grove School in 1946 when I was six years old," shared Candace Stockton. "My mother was a member of the PTA and my father served on the school board many of the years that I was going there," she added.

The same year Stockton began attending classes at the one-room schoolhouse, the small district received a special recognition that demonstrated the commitment of the teacher and the support received from the community in providing a quality educational experience for the students.

In 1946, the Harmony Grove School was honored for having gone from one of the poorest schools in Cole County to one of the best in an eleven-county area of Mid-Missouri. Earning a first-class rating of ninety-five, a report indicated that the high rating came from such initiatives as the addition of new reference books for the library, refurnishing of the school room, and the installation of electric lights.

"The Harmony Grove rural school was presented its certificate of first-class rating by County School Superintendent J.M. Wilson at a meeting of the Parent Teachers Association Monday night at the schoolhouse," the *Daily Capital News* reported on December 25, 1946. Stockton added, "We always got top honors when Genevieve Devine was the teacher—you learned to read and write through her no-nonsense approach, but she was able to do it in a very gentle way. She was my teacher from the first through fifth grades."

Soon discussions began shifting toward the consolidation of small, rural school districts, and in 1946, the County Board of Education met at Harmony Grove to discuss a proposed reorganization program for county schools. The beginning of the end for Harmony Grove came with Missouri's 1947 school reorganization law, placing it under the new "R-4 District."

The *Jefferson City Post-Tribune* explained in its edition from July 10, 1953, "R-4 became a reorganized district in 1949 when 10 school districts voted to go together as one identity and maintain schools at the six school buildings previously mentioned (which included the Harmony Grove schoolhouse)."

This legislation provided funding for many improvements to be made at Harmony Grove that included additional curriculum and physical fitness opportunities while also providing equipment such as projectors and phonographs. However, this represented an early step in consolidation that would later lead to the closing of many of the one-room schoolhouses around Jefferson City.

"Harmony Grove closed in 1953 when we were consolidated into the Jefferson City school district," said Stockton. "I was the only one in my class nearly all the years I went there and imagine the culture shock when I went into an eighth-grade class of two hundred students at Jefferson City," she recalled.

Transportation was provided to the centralized educational facilities. This new arrangement did provide many benefits to the former rural districts. The students now had educational and athletic opportunities previously not available to them.

"The R-4 school district will auction off the Harmony Grove School March 29," noted the *Sunday News and Tribune* on March 16, 1958. "The school is located on (Scruggs) Station Road."

In the years that followed, the schoolhouse was converted into a home and, following the addition, relocation, and renaming of area roads now sits on South Country Club Drive.

The closeness that developed among the students of the one-room schoolhouse, as they learned under the focused instruction of a lone teacher, became a slice of traditional Americana. It serves as a near-forgotten educational model that has provided many joyful memories and important lessons for several area residents.

"I just loved going to Harmony Grove School and I know that I received a fantastic, quality education there," Stockton maintained. "It's really such a shame that one-room school districts no longer exist because they taught us not only academic lessons but also patriotism, good values, and morals." *(Photographs courtesy of Candace Stockton.)*

Centennial School – Brazito area

Although records do not indicate when Centennial School opened, some area residents speculate its beginnings date back to 1876, at which time it took its name from the country's centennial celebration. This forgotten pillar of education—the one-room schoolhouse—stood near the junction of Oakland and West Brazito Roads in rural Cole County and is now remembered through assorted newspaper clippings and recollections of a former student.

"The re-union (sic) of the Cole County Union Sunday Schools gathered at Cole Spring Church (near Russellville) Thursday, August 7th," the *Osage Valley Banner* reported on August 14, 1879. "The meeting was called to order by instrumental music; and first, singing by Enterprise School. Second, speaking by A.G. Templeton, for Centennial School, and singing by said school," the newspaper added.

Twelve years later, in June 1891, Centennial School became one of three locations used by the school commissioner for Cole County to hold examinations for teachers seeking certificates to teach in the county's schools. Many educators began their extensive careers teaching classes in one-room schoolhouses such as Centennial, which was occasionally referred to as the Brazito Public School. However, there were other teachers who chose to leave the profession in pursuit of other employment possibilities.

Pictured is the class of Centennial School in a group photograph taken on February 1, 1892. John S. Lumpkin, far right, holding the bell, was a at the time the teacher. Lumpkin later became a deputy county clerk and county superintendent of schools. Courtesy of Randy Deuschle.

"Prof. N.R. McCamment of Brazito, Mo., has accepted the position of barber at the Tuckley barber shop, and assumed the duties this morning," the *Jefferson City Republican* printed on March 31, 1904. "Few people knew that Mr. McCamment was an experienced barber, but such is the case." The paper clarified, "He has been teaching the Brazito public school for a good many years but has finally decided to go back to his first love."

Bill Blochberger Sr. grew up near Centennial School, often making the journey on foot of more than two miles. While he was walking to classes, several of his fellow students would join him on the trek.

"I started at Centennial School in 1945 and went there for six years," Blochberger said. "If it was nice, we would walk and other times I would ride a bicycle. If the weather was bad, my mother would sometimes drive me there."

The rural schoolhouses not only served as a location for educational instruction but provided a centralized setting for medical-related activities. One such instance occurred in the fall of 1929 when Dr. W. Leslie of Russellville conducted physical examinations for the school's fifty students.

The *Jefferson City Post-Tribune* printed on April 20, 1929, "Brazito school, known as the Centennial School, has closed another successful term with Mr. Archie Russell as teacher, for the third year. He will again teach this school next year."

Archie Russell, a World War I veteran who also worked as a rural mail carrier, later taught at schools in Osage City, Cole Junction, and the Lohman area, prior to returning to Centennial School. While Blochberger was one of Russell's pupils, he also recalls other teachers during his time there including June Rudder and Mrs. B.A. Rogers.

"The last two years that I went to school there, the teacher was also the bus driver . . . using an old Chevrolet car," Blochberger explained. "I remember one time the weather had been cold and nasty. When we came up the hill by the school, the car did a 360-degree turn on the ice, but fortunately, we didn't crash."

As with many rural schools, local residents served as "directors," or the school board president. For a few years, this position was held by John Dawson, who lived on a farm adjacent to the Blochberger family. In earlier years, William Popp fulfilled the role of the school's director. The Centennial School also provided the setting for home cooking activities, such as the testing of gauges on pressure cookers in 1946. This event also included a presentation to local attendees on the best means to can, freeze, and preserve different foods.

Blochberger went on to finish the sixth grade at Centennial School in 1951 before transferring to Immanuel Lutheran School in Honey Creek for his seventh and eighth grade years. Following this, he finished his high school education at the public school in Eugene.

In 1953, Centennial School closed due to the consolidation of several rural districts in the area. The schoolhouse remained in its original location for only a couple of years.

"Sometime around the mid-1950s, Raymond Hogg moved the school to a piece of property near Hickory Hill to be used as a house," Blochberger said.

During the nation's bicentennial in 1976, Shirley Nelson helped draw pictures of historic buildings near the community of Brazito, which were then embroidered on a bicentennial quilt donated to the Cole County Historical Society. One of these sketches featured the exterior view of the former Centennial School.

By being remodeled into a home, Centennial School was blessed with a second life in a period when many other rural schoolhouses were demolished and forgotten. Though the property where it stood along West Brazito Road now stands bare, memories of the purpose it served remain fresh in Blochberger's mind.

"Basically, the teacher managed all the classes for first through eighth grade, and that was not something easy to do," he said. "Even though I only had three in my class at one time and there may have been a dozen students in the entire school while I was attending, those different levels of instruction weren't easy to manage. The school," he added, "is an important part of our local history and reflects a time when it was truly about remaining focused on the basics of education—reading, writing, and arithmetic." *(Primary photograph courtesy of Schellie Blochberger.)*

Archie Russell – Russellville area

Educator, soldier, rural mail carrier, and farmer are descriptions aptly defining the life of the late Archie Russell. Regardless of the capacity in which he served, he earned a reputation for being a dedicated public servant who lived his Christian values and strived to provide a good education to youth throughout several Mid-Missouri communities. Russell's origins began four miles south of Russellville when, in 1889, he became the first of five children born to John and Nannie Russell. In his youth, he attended nearby Cottage Grove and Proctor Schools but when his parents moved to a farm near Enon in 1905, he started classes at the one-room New Zion School.

"When he was young, he joined the Enon Baptist Church, where his mother was a charter member," said John Russell, Archie's grandson. "He was baptized in January 1909, and they had to cut eight inches of ice on the Moreau Creek for the baptism to take place," he added.

In a history printed for the Procter family, Archie Russell wrote, "In 1912, I finished the last part of my 8th grade year at Olean. I rode the train from Enon to Olean on Monday and then back to Enon on Friday." He continued, "During the week, I stayed with my Uncle Jim and Aunt Elizabeth Campbell."

According to Archie's grandson, John Russell, during his senior year at Olean, he passed the written examination to become a teacher and went on to attend the State Normal School in Warrensburg (now the University of Central Missouri). After one year at the school, he earned this teaching certificate. His new career commenced in 1914 at Cottage Grove School—a one-room schoolhouse three miles south of Russellville and where he had been a student several years earlier. As he approached the end of his second term of teaching at the country school, an unexpected event occurred.

"The building was completely destroyed by a tornado on the evening of April 19, 1916," explained the Russellville sesquicentennial book printed in 1988. "The building was blown against a large tree and demolished. A spelling bee was to be held at the school that evening, but the storm hit before anyone arrived."

While Cottage Grove was being rebuilt a short distance away, Russell taught a half-term at Sherwood School located 2-1/2 miles west of Russellville. However, in January 1917, he suspended his teaching career to pursue another public service career.

John Russell explained, "He bought a 1915 Model T Ford from a dealership in Jefferson City and was appointed a rural letter carrier for the Russellville area."

Three months later, the United States declared war against Germany, sparking yet another deviation in the experiences for Russell. Caught by the net of the military draft, he was inducted into the U.S. Army at Jefferson City on October 4, 1917, when twenty-seven years old.

Archie Russell served many years as a teacher at several public schools throughout Mid-Missouri in locations such as Russellville, Brazito and Osage City. He is pictured with his wife, the former Edith Flessa.

His family noted that during his training at Camp Funston, Kansas, his fellow soldiers, most of whom were several years younger, affectionately referred to Russell as "Grandpa." Assigned to Company I, 354th Infantry, his unit deployed to France in June 1918.

"I spent a total of 19 months in the service, 10 of which were overseas, but I was never in any battles," Russell wrote in later years. "They found out I had taught school and pulled me to . . . teach some of the other soldiers how to read and write . . ." He further explained that later in the war, his commanding officer appointed him "Town Major," giving him the responsibility of locating places for the company's soldiers to sleep and rest.

After receiving his discharge on April 25, 1919, he returned to Mid-Missouri and the following year married Edith Flessa of Centertown. He soon went back to teaching and remained at Russellville School until 1926, at which time he was hired at Centennial School near Brazito.

"Whenever he got a new teaching position, he rented a home for his family near the school," said his granddaughter, Jane Russell.

According to the July 1, 1929, edition of the *Jefferson City Post-Tribune*, Russell continued in his postal duties and was at the time delivering mail on the Brazito route. In later years, he also taught for three years at Osage City, one year at Cole Junction, and three years at Mt. Hope School near Lohman. In the 1930s, during the midst of the Great Depression, he purchased his parents' farm near Enon, where he and his wife raised their son and daughter.

Proud of his WWI service, Russell served as the commander of the American Legion Post in Russellville in the late 1940s. He also engaged in small-scale farming prior to retiring from teaching in 1947 and was an active member of Cole Spring Baptist Church near Russellville, teaching Sunday school classes for many years.

Even in his retirement years, he remained actively involved in activities related to education, serving on the school board in Russellville and as a member of a public library in Jefferson City. The retired educator was ninety years old when he passed in 1980 and lies at rest in Enloe Cemetery next to his wife, who succeeded him in death eight years later.

"He taught a lot of students over the years and when we were kids, we couldn't go anywhere with him that someone didn't know him," said Becky Russell, reflecting on the extensive life and career of her late grandfather. "He was very invested in children and their education was always a big part of his life." She added, "He simply enjoyed teaching." *(Photographs courtesy of the Russell family.)*

Surprise School – North of Russellville in Moniteau County

By the end of 1948, there were approximately 77 schools in Moniteau County, according to the 2000 edition of the book "Moniteau County Missouri History." Many of these schools were represented as the small, one-room schoolhouse with a single teacher. As the website SchoolMap.org notes, Moniteau County now has a total of six public school districts.

"Improved roads, newer, larger and more efficient buses, funding challenges, and the push to consolidate schools . . . contributed to the demise of the once highly cherished one room school," noted an article on the website of Missouri State University. "One room schoolhouses across the United States served not only as places to teach children reading, writing and arithmetic but as a community gathering place for business meetings and social events," the university explained.

Few schoolhouses have survived the decades, with most now being little more than broken relics of their former glory. Regardless, many of these buildings continue to hold fond memories for the now older adults who once attended them. Included in this extensive list is Surprise School, once located between Russellville and McGirk on State Highway K. For a number of years, it was the building where many local students received their basic instruction in a range of academic subjects.

"Since there weren't enough kids to open the nearest one-room school, I attended the first and second grades at California," said Norris Siebert, who was raised north of Russellville on Rockhouse Road. "But, starting the third grade in 1942, the powers that be decided to re-open the local one-room school."

The schoolhouse had burned to the ground years earlier, Siebert explained. It was so quickly rebuilt that it surprised many area residents, resulting in the decision to name it "Surprise School." In the years that followed, the schoolhouse hosted students who attended grades first through eighth. Like many of the students Siebert attended classes alongside, there was no transportation system in place and he had to daily make the walk to school.

"Even our teacher, Ellen Messerli, walked to the school but I think my distance was the furthest—2-1/4 miles," said Siebert. "Occasionally a car would come by and give me a ride, but that didn't happen often."

For eight years, Don Wyss attended the one-room Enon School. He remarked that since there was only one teacher, an alternating grade level was used so that the teacher did not have to instruct every grade each year.

"It fell to my lot to be a grade alternator," Wyss noted. "After grade four, I skipped to grade six, fell back to grade five, skipped to grade eight, and then fell back to grade seven, from where I graduated. That system now seems strange, but actually wasn't that bad."

Wyss was approached by Oscar Siebert and Guilford Heidbreder in 1947, both members of the board of the reopened Surprise School. They sought a new teacher and Wyss, eighteen years old with only twenty college hours, was offered the job. He attended summer courses at the college in Warrensburg and completed a ten-week workshop on teaching school.

Beginning his teaching career in the fall of 1947, Wyss explained, "At first, I wondered why anybody would teach school for a living, but I soon came to like it." He added, "The students were very capable, and, at the time, I did not realize that this would lead to a lengthy career in education."

One of the life-shaping experiences, Wyss recalls, came when a local woman sponsored a Jewish family that had been interred in a concentration camp in Germany during World War II. The family consisted of a young boy and girl. They both attended nearby Surprise School.

"The children spoke German but no English . . . and I couldn't speak German," Wyss recalled. "I wondered, 'How in the world can I teach them?' But I discovered they could do arithmetic very well and I would do a lot of object lessons, such as holding up a pencil and saying, 'This is a pencil,' while having them repeat after me."

Surprise School was located a few miles north of Russellville on State Highway K. Pictured is eighth-grade graduating class in the spring of 1949. From left: Donald Maples, Roger Kirchoff, Norris Siebert and their teacher, Donald Wyss.

In his first year, the eighth grade graduating class attended graduation ceremonies at nearby California, where Wyss was asked by the county superintendent of schools to introduce the speaker from the state department of education.

"I started to introduce the speaker and, because I looked so young, he thought that I was one of the eighth-grade graduates!" Wyss exclaimed. "I said, 'No, I'm the teacher!'" he chuckled.

Wyss made the daily drive to Surprise School from his home in Enon, earning a monthly salary of $175. Occasionally, the road to the school became so muddy and poor, that he parked his car at the home of Oscar Siebert, who then transported him and several students to the school on a wagon towed by his tractor.

In the spring of 1949, Norris Siebert was among the three graduating eighth-grade students at Surprise School. Reflecting on his education, he noted, "I am sure we were learning high school subjects, because when I got to Russellville High School (in the fall of 1949), it just seemed like a review of what I had already learned."

Don Wyss served three years as the teacher at Surprise School, stating the educational institution closed due to the consolidation of rural schools in 1950. He went on to spend more than four decades in education but recognizes his time in a one-room school provided some of the most important lessons of his career.

"Experience is the best teacher and I probably learned more at Surprise School about teaching and human nature than I learned from any university class." He added, "I really believed in the rural school structure, and it was a different education from the standpoint that you learned by doing ... learned to make the most of the resources available." *(Photograph courtesy of Norris Siebert.)*

Corinth School – South of Jefferson City near Zion

The Corinth School was a one-room brick schoolhouse that stood near the southwestern end of Zion Road in rural Cole County. Nearby was Loesch Road, so named for a family who had a long association with the school. This family not only had children who attended the school, but also some who served on the board and volunteered with various community organizations that later met in the building.

"The annual school meeting was held at the Corinth School Tuesday," the *Cole County Weekly Rustler* printed on April 8, 1927. "Edwin Loesch was elected as a new director," the newspaper added.

Candace Stockton explained that her father, Ernest Loesch, attended classes at both Cornith School and Zion Lutheran School while growing up on a nearby farm. He and his younger brother, Eddie, shared a story of a little unexpected entertainment they helped create for one of their teachers.

"My dad said that he and Uncle Ed always walked to school together and seemed to find a little trouble along the way, as young people tend to do," Stockton said. "Apparently on one Halloween,

they got a bunch of kids together and put the teacher's buggy on top of the outhouse." Chuckling, she added, "I don't think the teacher was pleased about it and was concerned because she didn't know how she was going to get home."

In 1947, this picture was taken at Corinth School of a book distribution to rural areas by the librarian from Jefferson City. The photograph was later featured in an international publication.

Lydia Huhn of Lohman was hired as the teacher for Corinth School in the late spring of 1920, with the board of directors approving her monthly salary for the coming term at $55 per month. The school became a training ground for many teachers throughout the years including Maurine George and Margie Fahrni-Schneider, the latter of whom also taught at schools in Enon, Russellville, and Jefferson City. In the spring of 1929, the rural school boasted one graduate, Pearl Ehrhardt.

"The Moreau Valley 4-H Club was chartered in 1932 and became one of the local community groups that held their meetings at Corinth School," said Stockton.

In 1934, Corinth School benefitted from a Great Depression-era economic recovery initiative called the Civil Works Administration. Through this program, workers installed "four new windows on the left side of the wall providing better lighted facilities for students," the *Sunday News and Tribune* reported on April 1, 1934.

After the end of the school session in 1945, when Candace Stockton had finally reached the age to begin classes where her father had attended years earlier, the Corinth School was closed because of the consolidation of local districts.

She said, "I began going to school at Harmony Grove near the fairgrounds (in Jefferson City), but fortunately the community came together to maintain the old Corinth School and used it as a building where they could continue holding meetings for local organizations like the Moreau Valley 4-H Club."

The schoolhouse would help create many fond memories for Stockton and other children of the community during the next several years.

"Helen Miller was the librarian in Jefferson City, and she would come out to the Corinth School and put on different educational programs when I was a kid," Stockton recalled. "Sometimes she would bring stacks of books with her that we could check out to take home to read."

One such visit resulted in a photograph being taken that not only showed Stockton and her father but was featured in an international publication printed by the United Nations Educational, Scientific and Cultural Organization (UNESCO).

According to the *Sunday News and Tribune* on October 15, 1950, the pictures, which were taken in 1947 inside the old Corinth School, "show Miss Helen Miller, Cole County and Jefferson City librarian, and members of rural club groups checking out books."

Stockton said, "Viola Smith was a Home Extension Agent with the University of Missouri Extension Office and would often put on programs at the Corinth School for the Cole County Extension Clubs." She continued, "There was also the Happy Hour Extension Club that met there but their members started getting older and couldn't do the activities necessary to maintain their certification. So, they eventually changed their name to the Happy Hour Neighbors Club and continued meeting at the school."

The community often gathered for workdays at the Corinth schoolhouse, completing all the necessary maintenance to keep the aging building in usable condition.

"I really enjoyed being part of the Moreau Valley 4-H that met there, but it dissolved in the early 1950s because there were only three of us girls attending since most of the boys were off in the military. Then, in the mid-1950s, it was combined with another group to form the Stringtown-Corinth 4-H."

During the 1960s, Stockton woefully recalled, use of the schoolhouse was discontinued following complaints from a local resident. The building was then sold and torn down. A private residence has since been built near the site where the school once stood. The Happy Hour Club continued to meet at private residences until the 1990s but eventually dissolved with the passing of its members. The Stringtown-Corinth 4-H Club continues to meet in the parish hall of St. John's Lutheran Church in Stringtown.

"I hated to see the Corinth School go because that's where my father attended school and where I spent so much time with my family and friends attending different group events," Stockton reflected. "It may have just been an old building, but it had become an important part of the community and the community was sad to see it torn down." *(Photographs courtesy of Candace Stockton.)*

Van Pool School – Northwest of Russellville

Decades ago, long before consolidation of school districts heralded their extinction, small schoolhouses were scattered across the local landscape, representing the primary means of education for students of many ages in rural communities. One of these small utilitarian buildings was known as the Van Pool School, quietly tucked within a forested area a short distance northwest of Russellville. Located along Van Pool Road in Moniteau County, both the road and nearby schoolhouse were named for the Van Pool family, who were among some of the earliest settlers to arrive in the Russellville area in the mid-1830s.

Established in the mid-1890s, the *Moniteau County, Missouri Family History Book* published in 1980 by the county's historical society notes that "(t)he first building was a log school up on a hill from the last schoolhouse in the valley or flat as most people call it."

The second schoolhouse, a small white structure, was like many rural schools of the period, hosting a handful of students from the local area. They generally included academic instruction through the eighth-grade level. This education was generally provided by a single teacher, referred to as a professor, who oftentimes pursued their own college education while also teaching.

According to an article appearing in the *Russellville Rustler* (bygone newspaper) on July 6, 1897, the composite of the student body provided the fodder for an interesting editorial containing bold predictions for the future with regard to gender equality.

"The annual report of commencement proceedings again reveals the fact that girl graduates outnumber their boy associates about four to one, and it is the exception when the honors of the class are not borne by the fairer and the frailer sex. Who can say what effect this will be upon the coming generation if this startling disproportion continues?" The newspaper added, "If the world is to be governed by mind instead of muscle, and we do not doubt it, can anything withstand the sure prophecy of present events, which clearly reveals that woman will be, at least, man's equal in home, in church, and in government."

Archie Reichel taught at Van Pool School for many years but later accepted a position with Kemper Military School in Boonville. Courtesy of Jeremy P. Amick

The student population may have wavered throughout the years, but in the fall of 1931, during the early stages of the Great Depression, the school system was thriving with a reported enrollment of thirty students. Oddly enough, a few months earlier, the school reported a single graduate.

At the time, McGirk native Archie Reichel was serving as the school's professor.

The Daily Capital News described Reichel as "one of Moniteau County's most popular teachers." However, despite a booming enrollment at such a small school while the nation was entering the Great Depression, the year 1931 may have been one of the most memorable for young Reichel since, in late October, he married the former Gladys Irwin of Kansas City.

Donn Schmoeger, who owns the property on which the former schoolhouse once stood, said, "Both my mother and father attended the small school. I can recall my father telling me that sometime between World War I and World War II, the teacher told all the students to bring their parents to school the next day." Grinning, he added, "Apparently, he wanted to discuss having the students speak in English rather than the German they had been using."

His father, Wilbert Schmoeger, a 1936 graduate of Van Pool School, would not only spend his lifetime farming in the same area where he attended classes but later volunteered to serve as one of the school's directors alongside other past graduates such as Herbert Wyss.

Archie Reichel, whether recognizing the upcoming consolidation of rural school districts or seeking a more robust salary than the $100 a month paid to his replacement at Van Pool School in the 1944-1945 school year, made the decision to accept a position teaching English courses at Kemper Military School in Boonville. He would go on to retire from Kemper after teaching from 1945-1973.

The popular former teacher of Van Pool School and his wife lived their remaining days as residents of Boonville, where they raised their three children. In addition to his career in teaching, Reichel served as president of the Missouri State Baptist Brotherhood.

Van Pool School closed in 1947 after it was consolidated into the school district in nearby Russellville. When Donn Schmoeger's family acquired the property on which the school sat in the early 1960s, the school building was still standing. Yet, as has been the fate of many a rural schoolhouse, it was torn down in the late 1960s since it had fallen into a state of disrepair. These days, all that remains of this once bustling schoolhouse are a handful of memories and a flat, wooded patch where the building stood. Nearby, there is also a thick slab covering an old cistern and a concrete pit on top of which sat one of the outhouses.

In later years, a painting was made of Van Pool School, which was acquired by Donn Schmoeger's father. This painting, Schmoeger explained, is a treasured possession and serves as a connection to his late father. Furthermore, it has become one of the only surviving links to the near-forgotten past of a small schoolhouse in the woods and an extinct component of the rural education system. *(Primary photograph courtesy of the Schmoeger family.)*

Ambrose School – Ambrose community near Brazito

Decades ago, before consolidation heralded their end, one-room schoolhouses were scattered across the rural countryside. These small structures served as a gathering place where young people in the surrounding areas came to receive a basic education. Oftentimes, if not torn down in later years, many of these schoolhouses, including the Ambrose School near Brazito, became meeting places for community groups and organizations. Details of the early history of the Ambrose School remain something of a mystery, but according to the family lineage research of Dr. Bill Ambrose, it begins with his great-great-grandfather, James Valentine Ambrose.

"My great-great-grandfather emigrated from England and bought his first farm (along what is now Tanner Bridge Road) in 1853," said Dr. Ambrose. "As an Englishman, he highly valued education and could read and write quite well."

His farm grew to 440 acres in size and was located in the vicinity of what became known as the "Ambrose Community." As the father of two sons and five daughters, James Ambrose built a schoolhouse where his children and others in the area could be educated, thus earning it the designation of Ambrose School.

Land in the area was parceled out and sold as James Ambrose grew older and it is suspected that the schoolhouse was moved at some point. James' oldest son, Thomas Jefferson Ambrose, would go on to raise a family of five boys and five girls, who later attended the school estab-

Emmeline Crede was an early leader of the local 4-H Club, which held meetings in the Ambrose School. Courtesy of Doris Engelbrecht

lished by their grandfather. Thomas' daughter, Bessie Pendleton, later taught at Ambrose School.

By the time the 1914 plat map for Cole County was printed, it shows the schoolhouse situated on the northernmost section of a farm owned by Martin J. Engelbrecht, a well-known blacksmith in Brazito. His son, Julius Engelbrecht, purchased the property in 1917 and it remains in the family through his descendants.

"We found sections of an old limestone foundation where we believed one of the earlier schools was located," said Kevin Engelbrecht, whose father, the late LeRoy Engelbrecht, attended Ambrose School along with his siblings. "The current schoolhouse is located a short distance from these foundation stones along what was once an old county road."

According to the June 5, 1976, edition of the *Daily Capital News*, the "Old Ambrose School . . . is the third to stand on the site since 1908 and belongs to the Eugene School District. It now serves as a community building for 4-H meetings and the like, having housed eight grades of students about 30 years ago."

In 1937, while the school was still being used to educate local children, the Peck-Away Woodpecker Club was established and began to meet in the schoolhouse. The following year, the club changed its name to the Ambrose 4-H Club. Julius Engelbrecht, who owned the farm where the current schoolhouse stands, was widely recognized for his efforts in building the 4-H club and guiding its students through various projects with the assistance of local resident Rosalyn Sappenfield. Emmeline Crede, a well-respected member of Friendens United Church of Christ in Brazito, also became an influential leader in the Ambrose 4-H while her father-in-law, Charles Robert Crede, served thirty-two years as clerk for the Ambrose School.

"During the past years Ambrose members have been engaged in many projects," reported the *Sunday News and Tribune* on October 4, 1970. "Some have pursued these projects beyond 4-H years; for example, the Trinklein family with their gardening project now produces many vegetables which are sold commercially."

Julius' sons, Martin, and LeRoy Engelbrecht participated in 4-H under their father's guidance and both were selected to attend the National 4-H Club Congress in Chicago. In later years, Martin and his wife helped operate the club for the benefit of their own children and others in the community.

The Ambrose School was wired for electricity in 1947 but such updates only came to benefit the 4-H Club. The same year, school enrollment dropped to only five students, and consolidation with nearby larger schools, such as Eugene School District, resulted in its closure.

Julius Engelbrecht's 145-acre farm became that of his sons, LeRoy and Martin. The brothers set aside ten acres where each of their families would live; LeRoy's section included the site of the most recent Ambrose School, which was built in 1908. The remaining 125 acres were then co-owned and farmed by both brothers.

"The Ambrose 4-H basically just faded away during the 1970s," said Doris Engelbrecht, LeRoy's widow.

The schoolhouse once set on a half-acre lot with an additional half-acre being donated in later years. The former school, along with the woodshed and two outhouses, remains standing on the one-acre property, although time has taken its toll on the historic structure.

"Several years ago, my husband and I approached the Eugene School District about purchasing the Ambrose School and the one-acre it sits on," said Doris Engelbrecht. "It was our understanding the property was to revert back to the property owner if it was no longer being used as a school and we were able to acquire it, which happens to be in the middle of our property," she added.

The building has become weathered in appearance, partially obscured by mature trees and growth. Regardless, the schoolhouse stubbornly endures as a testament to James Valentine Ambrose, one of the first settlers in the area, and his dedication to ensuring an education for area residents.

"There are certainly no plans to remove the school," stated Doris Engelbrecht. "My husband (who passed away in 2019) attended school there and so few of these historical schoolhouses still exist. This is part of the community and its history," she concluded. *(Primary photograph courtesy of Jeremy P. Ämick.)*

Osage Bluff School – *Osage Bluff*

The Osage Bluff School remains the only standing building denoting the existence of the community from which it took its name. In 1885, Osage Bluff had a reported population cresting 100 residents and boasted traditional rural businesses such as a blacksmith shop and a general store. The first school in the area, local resident Kenneth Braun noted, was a log building that was erected around 1895.

"That old school was located across from my home on Route B, about a quarter mile from here and set down in a holler," he said. "For whatever reason, they quit using it and there's nothing left of it now," he added.

But several years later, a new schoolhouse was built, which became Osage Bluff R-12. This durable, one-room structure survives to this day, thanks to the dedication of Braun and the suggestion of many neighbors who have since passed away.

"In the year 1905, a new school was built on the corner of Mathias Sommerer's farm," wrote Hazel Braun, Kenneth's wife, several years ago in a brief history of Osage Bluff. "Two barbecues and dances were held to pay for the building. Beer was a nickel and barbecue 50 cents."

Braun cut a large door in front of the schoolhouse so that he could use the building to work on automobiles but has striven to maintain its original exterior appearance.

She went on to write that the entire cost for erecting the new schoolhouse was $700 with the contractor being Christian Jacobs, whose father, John, was one of the pioneer residents of Osage Bluff. Also, the previous log school had been located on the farm owned by Christian Jacobs.

"The new schoolhouse that was constructed in 1905 had a

limestone block foundation and the exterior was made from cedar weatherboard," said Kenneth Braun. "In later years, they built a small wall along the north side of the building to block the windows, which created a narrow closet room."

According to Volume VII of the *Ohio Public Health Journal* from 1917, "The light in the modern school room should be admitted from one side only, and the seats should be arranged so the light is admitted at the left of the pupils. It has been found that this method of lighting is better adapted to school room needs . . ."

Braun explained, "Another interesting feature I discovered in the construction of the building is that they poured concrete five feet high inside the walls. Years ago, George Jacobs (son of Christian, the school's builder) told me that they did this since there was a lot of hunting in the area and they didn't want a bullet coming through the walls and striking a student."

For several decades, Osage Bluff R-12 School was the only public school in an area surrounded by parochial schools, such as those in nearby Wardsville and Honey Creek. In 1930, a midnight picnic was held at the Osage Bluff as a benefit for the school and, for many years, the schoolhouse served as a voting precinct for elections.

According to the *Miller County Autogram-Sentinel* in their edition printed May 21, 1942, Barbara Miller, a recent graduate of Eugene High School, had been hired as the teacher at Osage Bluff for the coming term. In 1945, Archie Smith was serving as the teacher and helped plan a dance to raise money in support of the war effort.

On February 22, 1947, the Osage Bluff 4-H was organized with Archie Smith serving as the first adult leader of the group. For years, the 4-H held meetings in the Osage Bluff schoolhouse until the group eventually disbanded.

"The school was closed in 1949 when it consolidated with the district in Eugene," said Kenneth Braun. "For a while, it continued to be used as a meeting spot by the 4-H, a coon hunting club, and the Osage Flood Control Association (the latter of which worked with the Corps of Engineers regarding the dam and flood prevention along the Osage River)." He continued, "When the school consolidated, what generally happened is many of the Protestants went to Eugene and the Lutherans to Honey Creek. If you were Catholic, you went to Wardsville." He added, "Some of the other students went to Osage Bend or Westphalia since they also had public schools."

Braun moved to the community of Osage Bluff in 1969, and the schoolhouse sat near his home on one acre that was still owned by the Eugene School District.

"Upon advice from the school's attorney, the board adopted a resolution to the effect that the school's interest in Osage Bluff School . . . was of no value and therefore, the board voted to issue a quit-claim deed to the current owners of the property . . ." reported the *Eldon Advertiser* on July 12, 1984.

"The property was deeded to Edna Sommerer, and I purchased the property from her," said Kenneth Braun.

Since that time, Braun has worked to restore the old schoolhouse, thus maintaining a tangible connection to a community that has all but disappeared. The building caught fire in 2017, but thanks to an alarm he had installed, the fire department arrived in time to save the historic building and the damage was soon repaired.

"When I first came to own the schoolhouse in 1984, I thought about tearing it down and putting up a big shed, but some of the old-timers from around here about had a fit over that," he said. "They were good neighbors and loved the schoolhouse, so I decided to keep it and cut a bigger door in the front so that I could use it as a shop. It is definitely an important part of Osage Bluff history and I guess you can say that I just fell in love with it over the years," he added. *(Photographs courtesy of Jeremy P. Ämick.)*

Lincoln School – South of Enon

On a privately-owned farm a short distance south of Enon stands the skeletal remnants of a clapboard structure once known as District 81, or Lincoln School. If you were to ponder its vast history, there might be visions of a small building blanketed in snow as a young teacher loads wood in a potbelly stove, before writing arithmetic problems on a large blackboard for students to solve.

Though it is uncertain as to the specific date Lincoln School was established, the 1980 edition of the *Moniteau County Missouri History* explains, "Old Timers have passed down the information that the first Lincoln School was a log building built around the time of the Civil War."

The schoolhouse was later moved approximately one-half mile to the southeast and, throughout the years, hosted a number of teachers. One of these was Gertrude (Snodgrass) Taylor, a native of Pisgah who married Enon resident Edgar Taylor on December 31, 1909.

"Mrs. Taylor taught several rural schools in the area as well as the Kansas City Business College when she lived in Independence," reported the *Eldon Advertiser* on February 14, 1985. "She retired from teaching at age 78 from Murphy Business College of North Hollywood, where she lived for several years," the newspaper added.

Though many women dedicated a portion of their youth to providing the best available academic instruction for students in the first through eighth grades, the educators at Lincoln School appeared to suffer from a litany of tragedies. In 1919, Lucy Hamlin of California, Missouri was employed to teach at Lincoln School and instructed there for several terms. However, she later married Charles Howar of Tipton and the couple moved to Los Angeles in 1931.

Lucy (Hamlin) Howar, pictured in 1919, was one of many young women who taught at Lincoln School during their careers in education.

"Charles E. Howar, a telephone company investigator, was exonerated by a coroner's jury late yesterday of blame in connection with the death of his wife, Mrs. Lucy Howar, who was killed by the accidental discharge of her husband's revolver Wednesday night," reported the *Illustrated Daily News* (Los Angeles) on December 30, 1933. "Howar told police that he had kept the gun under his pillow, following a burglar scare, and that it had been discharged when he pounded his pillow to make himself more comfortable," the paper went on to report.

Dorothy Hale Martie was another popular teacher who was employed at the school around the period of World War I. The High Point native later married and was only 22 years old when she died from accidental poisoning on April 17, 1921.

"Miss Vera Jenkins, who was teaching at Lincoln School and boarding at the home of A.E. Scott, had the misfortune Saturday night of getting badly burned," noted the *Eldon Advertiser* on February 8, 1923 edition. "She was taken to her home in Boonville . . . and accompanied by Dr. W.E. Martin who reports her to be in a critical condition."

Neva Walker would finish out the remainder of the term for injured Jenkins. In 1924, Mayme Scott passed her teachers' examination in nearby California and was appointed by the local school board to serve as the newest teacher for Lincoln School.

Several teachers provided the inspiration for others to fulfill their own desires to become educators. For instance, in May 1933, Grace Devore, a graduate of Olean High School, earned her teaching certificate at the Iberia Academy and received her first teaching job at Lincoln School. She would go on to teach at other schools around Enon, Marion, and Jamestown.

The next several years consisted of a medley of different teachers instructing for a few terms at Lincoln School before moving on to districts offering a better salary. A few local well-known teachers, such as the late Thelma Kraus and Dorothy Payne Hahn, were employed at the rural school during parts of their lengthy careers.

"I attended Enon School, which was located a short distance north of Enon, for all eight grades," recalled Don Wyss of Enon. "The entire time that I was there, Dorothy Hahn was my teacher." He continued, "Later when Dorothy Hahn transferred to Lincoln School, my mom decided to drive my younger sister there every day so that she could have Mrs. Hahn as a teacher. That is how respected she was as an educator around this community."

State consolidation laws eventually heralded the final blow to Lincoln School and several smaller districts throughout the state. In 1952, it was annexed into the Eldon school system with Dorothy Hahn earning the distinction of being the school's final teacher, having taught for the previous nine years in the small building.

These days, there are few who have any firsthand knowledge of the role one-room schoolhouses played in molding and educating young minds in the rural areas of the United States.

"The one-room schoolhouse was such an important part of education history," remarked Charles McGraw, former superintendent of the Blue Springs School District, in an article appearing in the *Kansas City Star* on June 11, 1998.

In an article by Bill O'Donnell shared by the National Park Service, one-room schools were not only viewed as the buildings where education was delivered but became an important part of the local communities in which they were located.

"Once a school was established in an area, it became sort of a focus. Children from the local area could meet each other and mingle. As they grew to know each other, a sense of belonging to a particular area grew." He added, "They were developing a sense of community." *(Photographs courtesy of Jeremy P. Amick.)*

***Margie Fahrni-Schneider – Corinth, Enon,
Russellville, and Jefferson City Schools***

Margie Farhni-Schneider was a beloved teacher who inspired many youths during the decades she spent in elementary education. Her teaching career began in the same types of one-room schoolhouses where she had received much of her early education. Several years later, she chose to selflessly invest both her heart and soul in providing a quality educational experience for the youth attending classes in the Russellville and Jefferson City School Systems.

Spending the first six years of her life in St. Louis, Margie's parents, Joe and Florence Procter, moved to a farm in the Enon area in 1931. As an only child coming of age during the Great Depression, she developed an abiding work ethic by helping with the chores around their property.

"I started to New Zion School in September 1931," Fahrni shared in her later years when describing the one-room schoolhouse near Enon. "There were three of us in first grade—Hershel Amos, Norman Amos, and me. Raymond Payne was the teacher," she added.

Her mother shared her Christian faith by attending Enon Baptist Church, where Margie accepted Christ as her savior in 1936. When not attending church functions or being involved in school activities, she recalled neighbors spending time visiting one another and enjoying such activities as playing rook, and checkers and savoring homemade ice cream.

She explained, "Now I was . . . out of school, wanting desperately to go to high school. Not everyone went to high school back then, in fact, very few did ... Now going to high school wasn't easy because the bus route didn't run any closer than Enon. I walked through the field, no matter the weather, before daylight, to meet the bus there."

The last few years of her education were fulfilled at Russellville High School, where Fahrni was recognized as the youngest member of her freshman class. In addition to her

Fahrni is pictured with her first husband, Freman, whom she married in 1944. Years after Freman's passing, she married a high school friend, LeRoy Schneider.

academic pursuits, she enjoyed playing basketball and participating in the "Pep Squad."

While still a senior, her interest in becoming an educator materialized after she was occasionally pulled from her classes to be a substitute teacher for the lower grades. Graduating as salutatorian of her class in the spring of 1941, Fahrni was awarded a scholarship to attend the Central Missouri State Teachers' College and completed classes during the summer months. Successfully completing the teachers' exams, Fahrni was sixteen years old in 1941 when she was hired for her first teaching position at the Corinth School—a one-room schoolhouse seven miles southeast of Jefferson City.

"I should add here that many applicants of Corinth School were men with families, and they couldn't live on the salary this little school could pay," she recalled. "I agreed to teach the eight months for $45 per month and paid Elmer and Jane Loesch $15 a month for room and board."

She continued attending college in the summer months and was hired back at Corinth School in 1942. The following year, she was hired at the salary of $90 a month as the sole teacher at Enon School, another one-room schoolhouse that was much closer to her parents' farm.

A young man name Freman Fahrni soon expressed an interest in dating Margie while she was teaching at Enon. The couple became engaged and were married during a small ceremony in California, Missouri, on July 27, 1944. They resided on a farm near Enon and, in 1948, welcomed their first and only child, a son they named Don.

Margie recalled, "Our lives went on pretty much the same as other couples. We attended Enon Baptist Church . . . We spent a lot of time with our little boy and about as soon as he was out of diapers, his dad started taking him to livestock sales."

Experiencing financial difficulties because of agricultural conditions in the area, the Fahrni family moved to Kansas City in 1951.

For the next three years, Freman worked for General Motors in a program supporting the F-84 Thunderjet—an American fighter-bomber aircraft. When the program was discontinued in 1955, they returned to the Enon area. For the next eleven years, Margie worked for the Russellville School System, primarily teaching fourth-grade classes. She also made the decision to return to college and finished her bachelor's in education at Lincoln University in 1958.

"Russellville School only had one teacher for each grade and if there were forty or more in that grade, one teacher had them all," she said.

She later applied for a job with the Jefferson City Public School System, teaching several years at Thorpe Gordon Elementary and finally retiring in 1980 with thirty-one years of teaching credit. Maintaining the dedication to her faith, in 1970 she transferred from Enon Baptist Church to Corticelli and remained active in the congregation.

Freman, her husband of fifty-three years, passed on in 1997. She continued to live a life of service to others through her church and by volunteering at St. Mary's Hospital. On February 21, 2004, she married LeRoy Schneider, with whom she had attended school in Russellville decades earlier. On December 11, 2014, the eighty-nine-year-old Margie Fahrni-Schneider passed away and was laid to rest alongside many friends and extended family in Enloe Cemetery near Russellville.

The stories of those she has inspired are often still shared around the Enon, Corticelli, Russellville, and Jefferson City communities. They describe a woman who left behind many heartfelt memories.

"She always found some way to compliment us," said Steven Smith, who was a fourth-grade student of Farhni's during the 1962-1963 school year. "She helped each one of us to master a subject to the best of our abilities, but her greatest attribute was loving us." He added, "Later in life, she was a precious friend."

DeeEllen Atkinson, who attended church with Fahrni in Enon, added, "I vaguely remember she had several health issues and when I visited her in the hospital, she was so uplifting with her faith . . . even with her illness, which spoke volumes to me. She and her family were such pillars in the community and strong individuals who shared their love for the Lord. I can't express how many youths she inspired during her life." *(Photographs courtesy of Don Fahrni.)*

Marie Wood – *Russellville and California High Schools*

Marie Wood has provided encouragement in the lives of thousands of students she taught during her four decades as an educator at high schools in Russellville and California. These experiences resulted in unexpected recognition from her peers and have gifted her with many wonderful memories upon which to reflect in her retirement years. Born on her father's birthday on August 16, 1928, Wood was raised on her parents' farm southwest of High Point. She attended a one-room schoolhouse known as Prairie Hill School through the eighth grade and then transferred to Eldon High School, where she graduated in 1946.

"I knew some people that had enrolled in Draughons Business School in Springfield, so I decided to go there as well," she said. "The program was about a year long if I remember correctly."

Following her graduation from the program, which provided instruction in several basic business skills, Wood was hired as a clerk for the Institutional On-Farm Training Program under the Missouri Department of Education in Jefferson City. The program assisted World War II veterans who were interested in pursuing careers in agriculture.

Wood recalled, "After about a year and a half, I decided to return to school and earned my associate's degree at Southwest Baptist College (now University) in Bolivar. When I graduated, I returned to the Missouri Department of Education, but this time as a secretary for the Director of Home Economics," she added.

Two years into her second stint with state government, Wood took the final step toward the completion of her educational goals by enrolling in college at Warrensburg. She went on to earn her bachelor's degree as she prepared to embark upon her career in education.

"The superintendent from Russellville came to Warrensburg in 1955 and interviewed me for a teaching position at the high school," she said. "I was hired to teach commerce courses—they were essentially business classes such as accounting, typing, and bookkeeping," she added.

For the next several years, she taught vocational business classes at Russellville High School while embracing other opportunities such as serving as a class sponsor and accompanying students on senior trips. She also found enjoyment in working closely with her students, helping to guide those who demonstrated specific aptitudes and interests.

"I was in her typing and bookkeeping classes," said Ron Klatt, a 1964 graduate of Russellville High School who went on to retire from a career with Central Bank in Jefferson City. "She encouraged me to pursue a profession in business and I am forever grateful for her guidance."

On other occasions, she observed certain students whose boundless energy and personalities have become imbued in her memory.

During her forty-two years of teaching business classes at the high schools in both Russellville and California, Marie Wood estimates she instructed around 4,000 students, many of whom went on to complete successful careers in business.

"I always remember the way Johnny Campbell answered a question that I asked in one class," she smiled. "I asked him what a semicolon was—meaning how it was to be used. He responded, 'It's a comma with a period.'" Pausing, she added, "He wasn't wrong; I guess I just worded the question in a confusing fashion. But he was certainly an ambitious and outgoing young man ... just full of life."

Johnny Campbell graduated from Russellville High School in 1964. A little more than three years later, he was killed while serving in Vietnam with the Marine Corps.

She added, "He was the type of person that would go right into battle and not try to avoid it."

In 1967, after having taught at Russellville for nearly twelve years, she was hired to teach business-related courses for California High School. As she explained, she chose to make the move to California since it would allow her to be closer to her parents.

As noted in the *Moniteau County, Missouri History* book published in 2000, during the school years of 1986-1987 and 1993-1994, Wood was bestowed the honor of being selected as Outstanding Educator of the Year by fellow faculty members.

She completed thirty years at California High School, retiring in 1997 with a total of forty-two years of teaching to her credit. In the years following her retirement, she became involved in many volunteer opportunities throughout the community. In 2001, she was elected the Distinguished Retired Teacher by the Morgan/Moniteau County Retired Teachers Association.

"Since retiring Marie has kept busy working with the Daughters of American Colonists (DAC), OATS and Moniteau County Historical Society," reported the *Tipton Times* on May 17, 2001. "Marie is a member of the First Baptist Church of California."

Accolades continued for the retired teacher when she was recognized as the OATS volunteer of the year for Moniteau County in the spring of 2005. OATS Transit is a nonprofit corporation providing transportation for rural residents, senior citizens, and persons with disabilities.

The hindsight that comes during our retirement years has not diminished the appreciation Wood possesses for her chosen career path. She has many fond memories that, at any given moment, can deliver comfort and boost her spirits.

"I can't say that I disliked any of the courses I taught but I really enjoyed teaching accounting," she said. "It was an interesting class to teach because I liked to see how everything fit together . . . especially when the students came to understand it." She concluded, "And in all of the years that I taught, I can't say that I had any disrespectful students in my classes. During my career," she smiled, "I taught about 4,000 students and thought of every one of them as 'my kids.'"

Marie Wood was ninety-three years old when she passed away on May 26, 2022, and was interred in the California Masonic Cemetery. *(Photographs courtesy of Jeremy P. Ämick.)*

Celia (Seidel) McIlwain – Russellville Elementary School

Celia (Seidel) McIlwain was for years a beloved fourth-grade teacher at the elementary school in Russellville who helped inspire generations of students. When she died unexpectedly from an automobile accident, an entire school district mourned, flooding to her funeral service to pay their final respects. Decades later, her memory is still celebrated by friends, family, and former students.

Born in 1951, Celia Seidel was the second of three children raised on a small farm on Meadows Ford Road north of Lohman. In her youth, she attended Centertown School through the eighth grade before transferring to high school in Jefferson City.

"On our parents' farm, we raised some cattle and put up a lot of hay," said McIlwain's older brother, Mervin Seidel. "We also grew some truck patches so Celia spent a lot of time helping Mom around the house and doing some canning of the vegetables we grew."

Church was also an important aspect of their family circle. The Seidels were members of the Central United Church of Christ in Jefferson City, where Celia underwent her Confirmation as a young woman.

Mervin, who was five years older, recalled that he and his sister had their moments of sibling rivalry and mirthful retaliation while growing up. On one occasion, when he was fifteen years old and Celia just ten, they played a game of croquet in the yard and had a disagreement on the rules.

"I kept knocking her ball across the yard and we argued about it for a little bit and then finally quit playing," he said. "We were walking back to the house and she came up behind

McIlwain is pictured in her senior photograph from 1969.

143

me and hit me in my upper back with the croquet mallet." Chuckling, he added, "That hurt for a while."

After graduating from Jefferson City Senior High in 1969, Celia enrolled at Lincoln University to pursue a degree in education. During college, she met Ralph McIlwain and they were married at Central United Church of Christ on June 2, 1973. A few weeks later, she graduated with her bachelor's degree in elementary education and was hired to teach the fourth grade at Russellville Elementary School.

"Although she loved to teach, I think she also wanted a career with the summers off because she loved outdoor activities like gardening," said Cheryl Morris, McIlwain's younger sister. Morris continued, "She was a Christian and her family was very important to her. The summer months were also a time for her to volunteer with her church at events like Vacation Bible School."

McIlwain and her husband became parents to a son and daughter—Matthew and Jill. Sadly, in 1987, they lost a son, Addison, in infancy. This proved to be an emotionally trying period for the McIlwain family, but through the support of relatives and friends, she continued to focus on her career and providing a quality education for her students.

Jim Kilson, a student of McIlwain's in the late 1980s, said, "She was always willing to go the extra mile to help those who were struggling by coming in early or staying late. She had a way of making learning fun to the point that even when it came to the difficult things, we were all on board to do it." He continued, "For me personally, I really struggled as a student when I was younger and those things made all the difference in the world."

On many occasions, McIlwain carpooled with other teachers who lived in the Jefferson City area. On November 27, 1989, the first Monday after the Thanksgiving holiday, she and three other teachers finished the school day at Russellville and were returning to Jefferson City when the unexpected occurred.

McIlwain was riding in a vehicle driven by one of her co-workers that was traveling eastbound on Route C. A car failed to stop at the intersection of Routes C and D north of Lohman and the vehicle in which McIlwain rode was struck on the left side, knocking it off the road.

"One Russellville teacher was killed and three were injured in an accident that occurred at 4:30 p.m.," reported the *Eldon Advertiser* on November 30, 1989. "Celia McIlwain of Jefferson City was pronounced dead at Charles E. Still Hospital."

Of the three teachers injured in the accident, only two were able to return to their careers in education.

"The superintendent got a call that some of our teachers were involved in an accident," said Jay Acock, who was at the time elementary principal at Russellville. "He came and got me, and we drove to the intersection, but it was all over by then. We knew that Peggy (Heinrich) and Celia were hurt bad, but I didn't hear that Celia had died until visiting the hospital a little while later."

Acock noted that counselors were brought in from Jefferson City to be available for students and faculty coping with the trauma of McIlwain's death and the medically-necessitated absence of the other teachers.

Funeral services for the thirty-eight-year-old McIlwain were held at Central United Church of Christ, where friends, family, and scores of students and faculty from Russellville Elementary School packed into the building. She was then laid to rest in Riverview Cemetery, the same location where her infant son had been interred two years earlier.

"It was not a good time in a lot of peoples' lives; it affected more than just family," said Morris. "But people obviously liked her and I know that she helped make a positive difference in a lot of lives.

My sister," she continued, "was a visionary and knew that her students could accomplish certain things academically. Then, through her imagination, she worked to make that vision become a reality."

Reflecting on his former teacher, Jim Kilson added, "She was super encouraging and often I'd hear, 'I know you can do this—give it another try!' And I know others heard it as well. She believed in us even if we didn't believe in ourselves." *(Photographs courtesy of Mervin Seidel.)*

Don Buchta – Blair Oaks School

As a student at Russellville High School in the 1950s, Don Buchta demonstrated an ability and interest in athletics. His success in sports earned him a college scholarship, which soon launched his career in education and resulted in his coaching several talented young athletes, one of whom went on to play baseball in the major leagues.

Born near Lohman in 1937, the oldest of two sons of William Buchta and Alma Koestner, Don spent his first year at Mt. Hope School—a one-room schoolhouse that closed when it consolidated with the Russellville School District. In 1955, he graduated from Russellville High School and decided to attend a nearby college.

"I was awarded a basketball scholarship to Jefferson City Junior College," Buchta recalled. "It was a two-year college and I earned an associate's degree there."

Buchta was among the last group of students to receive their diplomas from Jefferson City Junior College when graduating in the spring of 1958. Lincoln University, a historically Black college, had recently opened its doors to all students, leading to declining enrollment and the closure of the junior college.

Maintaining an interest in a career in education, he transferred to nearby Lincoln University, working on his bachelor's degree and then pursuing graduate work. In 1962, he was awarded a master's degree in education.

"I had family in Montana so I traveled there to do some graduate work for a couple of summers at the University of Montana and Montana State," he recalled. "Southwestern Montana had the best trout fishing in the nation and was probably the closest thing to heaven on Earth that I know of," he grinned.

He was offered a teaching job with the school district in Montgomery City and spent one year coaching boys' and girls' sports at the junior high and high school levels. Then, in 1963, he accepted a position at Waynesville, remaining there as a coach for the next three years. In 1966, Buchta heard that the new Blair Oaks School in Wardsville was under construction, and the school board was in the

Meyer is pictured in 1953 when graduating from the eighth grade at High Point. Her future husband, John Meyer, stands behind her.

process of hiring teachers. He contacted the school's superintendent and was told to visit with the school board president, Henry Boessen, for an interview.

"Boessen lived on a farm in the area and when I got to his house, his wife said he was down in the bottoms planting corn," said Buchta. "I drove down this old dusty road and found him, and then leaned against his tractor while he interviewed me." Buchta continued, "He asked me if I was Catholic and I told him that I was Lutheran. He paused for a second and said, 'Well, I have some friends that are Lutheran and they are good people.'"

Buchta was hired to teach social studies, English, and physical education. After starting the new job, he learned he was the only non-Catholic faculty member employed at the new school and only one of the students was not Catholic. These demographics, he added, began to shift as the public school grew in the coming years.

"When we reported in the summer of 1966, the school was still under construction and there wasn't even water available. They had to ship it in," he said. "The first year, they only had the ninth and tenth grades. The next year they added juniors and the third year they added the senior class.

He began coaching the freshman basketball team and recalls the gym floor being tile, requiring him to paint lines on the floor before games. He also coached baseball and cross-country while William "Skip" Rich was later hired to coach the new football team.

A memorable moment unfolded in the fall of 1972 when a young freshman from the Taos area arrived at the school and joined the baseball team, aptly demonstrating his impressive pitching abilities.

"Tom Henke and John Rackers were the two best players that I coached," recalled Buchta. "Henke could throw hard, had a heck of a fastball, and pitched for me until 1976. I pitched him probably every other game but we didn't play as many games back then as the schools do now."

Buchta earned his associate's degree from the former Jefferson City Junior College before transferring to Lincoln University. *Courtesy of Don Buchta*

Henke was later drafted by the Texas Rangers, became a relief pitcher for the Toronto Blue Jays, and finished out his major league career with the St. Louis Cardinals.

During a recent interview, Henke explained, "Coach Buchta was always right there trying to instruct us because we were pretty raw when he got us. He understood and recognized talent better than I ever could have and was always watching me pitch, telling me how to improve my delivery and get it in the strike zone." Henke added, "He always taught a good work ethic and that's what got us through."

Buchta served several years as Blair Oaks' athletic director before retiring from active teaching in 1986. He briefly substituted at area schools and then retired for good to live and work on his parents' farm near Lohman. His long-time friend and confidante, Shari Wolf, passed away in 2017; his younger brother, Roger, a retired teacher from Russellville High School, died unexpectedly in 2019.

In recent years, Buchta has stayed active by exploring caves throughout Mid-Missouri, remaining committed to his Lutheran church as a member of St. Paul's in Lohman, and reveling in discussions about local history.

While highlighting his career as a coach and teacher, Buchta remarked, "I loved sports and had some really good athletes play for me throughout my career. Watching students like Tom Henke and John Rackers improve and move up to the next level was a great enjoyment to me." He added, "That was the main reason I stayed in education and coaching for all of those years." *(Primary photograph courtesy of Jeremy P. Ämick.)*

Beverly Meyer – Russellville Elementary School

Small in stature yet a titan in spirit, Beverly Meyer has created a notable legacy through music education programs in several school districts. Though now retired, her boisterous nature continues to be felt in many communities through her volunteerism and charity seeking to ensure future generations remain proud of the sports and music programs at their schools. Born and raised on her parents' farm in High Point, Meyer not only learned to embrace the agricultural lifestyle at a young age but worked many hours in the J.F. Tising & Sons Store founded by her great-grandfather.

"It was a general store that opened in 1874," she recalled. "I was twelve years old when I first started working there and used to sweep floors, stock shelves, make change for the customers, and candle the eggs," she added.

Coming from what she described as a "musical family," Meyer took piano lessons from a woman who lived across the street and also participated in gospel singing groups as a child. Additionally, while attending the one-room schoolhouse in High Point, she and her fellow students received an introductory level of music education from their teacher.

"There's never been a point when I haven't had music in my life," she said.

After finishing the eighth grade at High Point, she transferred to California High School

Meyer is pictured in 1953 when graduating from the eighth grade at High Point. Her future husband, John Meyer, stands behind her.

and graduated in 1957. Clinging to an interest in teaching music, she enrolled at Central Missouri State College in Warrensburg.

"My aunts had gone to the college and my grandfather had attended there back when it was the [State] Normal School," Meyer said.

Meyer graduated with her bachelor's degree in music education in 1961. In the fall of that year, she was hired as a vocal and instrumental instructor for grades first through twelfth at Green Ridge R-8 southwest of Sedalia. Remaining there for the next twelve years, she led the choir and girls' glee club in earning the top score out of 23 schools participating in a contest. In 1972, she married John Meyer, with whom she had attended school at High Point, and the couple moved to Mid-Missouri.

"For three years, I taught school for one-half day at High Point and a half-day at Versailles," she said. "It was a very busy time because we were trying to build a house and I was also working at my father's store and giving piano lessons." She continued, "In 1975, I had to go to Russellville to make a house payment and while I was in the area, stopped by the school to see if they needed any help. I talked to the secretary for Grover Snead, who was the superintendent at the time, and told her I was interested in teaching."

The following day, Meyer received a call from Superintendent Snead, who said he had a contract waiting for her if she was still interested in a teaching position.

During the next quarter century, her music instruction for elementary classes included developing programs for PTO meetings, Thanksgiving, and Christmas in addition to assisting with the production of the Robin Hood musical. In 1999, her choir was invited to sing for a Christmas dinner at the Governor's Mansion, where she was presented a signed proclamation by Governor Mel Carnahan.

"We had a lot of fun in our classes," she said. "We even did the limbo and learned how to square dance," she grinned.

Years earlier, in 1990, she made the decision to close her father's store, realizing she could not both manage it and remain focused on her full-time employment as an educator. After retiring from Russellville in 2000, she continued teaching part-time for three years at the school in Latham. Well-earned recognition came in 2006 when she was among six educators—three of whom were from Russellville—selected as Missouri "Pioneers of Education." Sadly, the joy from these accolades was tempered by the passing of her husband, John, in 2009.

For years, she has lived on her family's farm, which has earned the distinction of being a "Missouri Century Farm." She made the decision to sell her father's store in 2016; however, her family's legacy in the community is sustained through Meyer's generosity to music and sports initiatives.

"One of my greatest enjoyments is volunteering to help out with the choir at Russellville," she explained. "In 2014, the choir earned a '1' in competition, something they hadn't done since 1966." With a smile, she added, "Back in 1966, my sister was the teacher, so that is an interesting connection." Meyer continued, "I also like playing the piano at school events like the program they put on for Veterans' Day. Also, I sell tickets at the ball games at Russellville and get to see many of my former students that way."

In recent years, her philanthropic spirit has been demonstrated by the purchase of pianos for the schools at High Point, Russellville, Latham, and California. Her generosity also includes donations made toward the purchase of the marquee for Russellville High School, band uniforms, and mascot-printed backboards for the school's gymnasium.

Although she and her late husband never had children of their own, Meyer recognizes that her career in education, along with voluntary endeavors, has earned her a family that numbers in the thousands.

"I have heard from several former students who ended up becoming music teachers," she said. "I guess that this might be a hint that I was a good teacher who influenced the lives of others . . . something that I just love." Meyer added, "And even if I never had children of my own, I know that I really have about 10,000 because of all those kids I have taught through the years, and that is pretty special to me." *(Photographs courtesy of Beverly Meyer.)*

CHAPTER 4

Business

Dixie Gardens - Centertown

When plans were being made in 1925 to expand the network of interstate highways in the United States, visionaries eyed opportunities to build businesses to serve the coming increase in tourism and traffic through their communities. In the small settlement of Centertown, the expanded road system inspired one individual to create a dance hall that for years remained a popular tourist destination and even welcomed rising stars to its stage. U.S. Highway 50 was a construction project that helped link Kansas City and St. Louis, passing through Centertown, in the mid-1920s. As the highway commission asserted, these ambitious road projects had the potential to yield great benefits to area residents.

"This means new business—a new garage, filling station, etc.," remarked highway officials in an article appearing in the *Tipton Times* on December 25, 1925. "Travelers will need to be fed and housed, and more and better . . . facilities and accommodations will follow. Cafes and restaurants will spring up."

By 1927, Centertown was thriving because of the traffic on the highway. With a population of fewer than three hundred residents, it boasted—among other businesses and organizations—churches, a school, two garages, two manufacturing plants, two grocery stores, a grain elevator, and two boarding houses.

Observing economic opportunities unfolding in the small community because of the access offered by the new U.S. Route 50, George W. Greene, a fuel distributor from Jefferson City and owner of service stations in the area,

The small cabins pictured were among several available for rent at Dixie Gardens. They have since been torn down due to deterioration.

chose to expand his business holdings to the Centertown area.

"The opening of beautiful 'Dixie Gardens,' located just west of Centertown on Highway 50, has been set for Wednesday evening . . . by builder and owner, George W. Greene," printed the *Jefferson City Post-Tribune* on Saturday, November 22, 1930. The newspaper continued, "The plans for the first night at this pleasure resort include a dance and high-class entertainers that have been booked by Mr.

Greene, and he extends a cordial invitation to the general public for the opening night."

The resort consisted of a log cabin structure measuring an impressive fifty by seventy feet and housing two private dining rooms, booths, and a dance floor large enough to accommodate 125 couples. Additionally, the main cabin had a dark walnut interior finish in addition to steam heat and a large fireplace.

Lucille Rosenmiller, a native of the Centertown area and local historian, explained, "They also built several small log tourist cabins near the main building where people could stay overnight. They were not very large barely big enough to fit a cot inside," she added.

Businesses, clubs, and fraternal groups flocked to use Dixie Gardens for dinners and social events. In 1931, Greene began serving lunch and dinner daily at the clubhouse and, on Wednesday and Saturday nights, welcomed couples willing to pay $1.00 to dance to the music of small bands and orchestras he hired.

Greene hired local resident Frank Wagner and his wife to help manage the daily affairs of Dixie Gardens while popular bands such as "Hack and His Rhythm Kings" continued to provide the entertainment for guests.

"Frank Wagner will have his filling station completed in the very near future; it will be located at the Dixie Gardens," noted the *Jefferson City Post-Tribune* on September 24, 1931. The newspaper continued, "Frank says no city tax on gas out there. Many will take advantage of the opportunity to save that amount."

In late summer 1932, two years after Greene built Dixie Gardens, he sold the business to Leroy E. Leonard of Windsor, a fellow oil and gasoline distributor interested in owning and operating a dancing and dining establishment.

The Great Depression, though defined by financial hardships, did not hinder the popularity of Dixie Gardens as a destination. Groups from throughout Mid-Missouri continued to rent the large building and its outside pavilion for assorted events, which, after the repeal of Prohibition in 1933, included the sale of alcoholic beverages.

The business was later sold to Ernest Mankin, who witnessed a lull in activities during World War II because of rationing and the scores of young men away for military service and unavailable to attend large dances. But after the war, activities continued at full pace with orchestras entertaining dancers, $1 chicken dinners, and the sale of beer and whiskey. On May 15, 1947, the young comedian Sid Caesar performed at the rural club, providing entertainment to a local crowd prior to achieving national stardom. But the post-war reemergence of the entertainment venue was soon to reach its end.

"Dixie Gardens ... was destroyed by fire last night in a spectacular blaze visible nine miles away at California [Missouri]," reported the *Sedalia Democrat* on August 6, 1947.

Lucille Rosenmiller noted, "I can remember my parents taking me up there the night that it burned. I was only a child at the time, but I can still see it burning in my thoughts all these years later."

The business was not rebuilt, the nearby gas station has since become a home and the small visitor cabins have been torn down. All that remains of its legacy is a private drive sign printed with "Dixie Gardens" on the western edge of Centertown.

In an article appearing in the *Eldon Advertiser* on September 15, 1988, the late Bob Richardson reflected on his past experiences at the club, "The spring I dated Jeanne Spalding, I tried to impress her by taking her to Dixie Gardens . . . It was a large and prestigious place that looked like an old Southern plantation. No jukebox, there was a live band." He added, "Nevertheless, Dixie Gardens was a class place . . ." *(Photographs courtesy of Lucille Rosenmiller*

Lohman Hotel and Saloon - Lohman

On Front Street in Lohman is a white, two-story block building that has been ravaged by the passing years. It is one of several early structures in the historic German Lutheran settlement, standing as evidence of the days of the former railroad spur known as the Bagnell Branch and notable figures connected to several Missouri communities.

Little is known about the actual date the building was constructed, but photographs maintained by the late Gert Strobel show that the remaining section of the building began as a hotel. Its south entrance faced the railroad depot. Attached to its west side was a wooden section that served as the primary saloon in Lohman. The saloon's story begins in the nearby community of Centertown, where John L. Blochberger, a native of Germany, settled and raised a family. Along with working a farm and operating a blacksmith business, he revealed an entrepreneurial spirit later embraced by his children.

According to the *Sedalia Democrat* printed on July 27, 1900, "The Centertown Milling company, of Centertown, Mo.; capital stock, $5,000" was incorporated by "J.J. Opal, John F. Flessa, John L. Blochberger . . . and others."

John Blochberger raised his family in the Lutheran faith and had, years earlier, joined many of his business partners in establishing the Emanuel Lutheran Evangelical Church in Centertown, which no longer exists. A cemetery is all that remains of this church and is now maintained by St. Paul's Lutheran Church in California.

"Lohman's bank, the Farmer's Bank of Lohman, was incorporated in 1909, with a capital stock of

This is the section of the old hotel that exists today. The saloon was located on the west side of the structure, which is now an open grassy area. Courtesy of Jeremy P. Amick

$12,000 . . ," noted a historical booklet printed about Lohman in 1976. The first Board of Directors included the following: [Frank] W. Blochberger, William Niederwimmer, John Scheperle, J.A.N. Linhardt, J. Henry Kautsch, [Andrew Siegel] Blochberger, and William S. Meyers.

While his brothers were establishing their foothold in the community of Lohman and following their father's entrepreneurial example, a younger William J. Blochberger was making his own mark in Benton County.

"W.J. Blockberger (sic), who has been conducting a saloon, known as the 'Arcade,' at Cole Camp, for the past four or five years, has just had his place improved in many respects, until he now has one of the finest furnished places of business in Central Missouri," reported the *Sedalia Democrat* on April 3, 1900.

The newspaper added, "'Block,' as he is known by his friends, who are legion, has given the people of Cole Camp the finest furnished saloon in the county . . ."

Two years previous, in 1898, William Blochberger married Elizabeth Heinrich, who was also from Centertown. The couple later became parents to a son and a daughter.

His experience in the saloon business, along with the relationships his older brother Frank established in Lohman while serving as a blacksmith and being actively involved in local political matters, inspired his decision to purchase the Lohman saloon sometime around 1901. The saloon was a two-story building connected to the white brick structure that served as a hotel for those traveling to and through the once-bustling railroad town. Photographs from the early 1900s show a clean, well-stocked establishment that demonstrated the pride William Blochberger took in his business.

Prior to purchasing the saloon in Lohman, he sold his business in Cole Camp and continued to pursue mining interests. Historical documents imply that he only operated the saloon for a few years, selling it around 1906 and moving to Sedalia. It was in his new Pettis County community that he operated both a bar and formed a company that distributed wholesale liquors.

The *Sedalia Democrat* reported on October 4, 1908, "The largest firms of the United States in different lines are located or represented here and among the notable concerns . . . [is] the Fred Miller Brewing Company of Milwaukee, whose representation in a wholesale way is W.J. Blochberger." It further explained, "This gentleman handles a very large trade, supplying the Miller Beer to practically all the local retail liquor dealers as well as enjoying a very large club and residential trade."

Sad news visited Blochberger when his wife, Elizabeth, was diagnosed with tuberculosis. She traveled to New Mexico in 1909 in hopes that the weather would be better for her health. She was thirty-nine years old when she died on February 7, 1910; her body was returned to Missouri and laid to rest in the Emanuel Lutheran Evangelical Cemetery in her native community of Centertown.

Blochberger again experienced emotional hardship when his older brother Frank, who had helped him in the business trades in Lohman years earlier, died on April 25, 1910. He lies at rest in the cemetery of St. Paul's Lutheran Church in Lohman. For the next decade, William Blochberger remained involved in mercantile interests in and around Sedalia but succumbed to pneumonia in 1920 when only fifty-two years old. He was laid to rest alongside his wife in Centertown.

After selling his interests in Lohman, the former saloon and hotel became a home for the Strobel family. The wooden section that was the saloon later caught fire and was removed, leaving only the block building that had been the hotel. This section eventually became the post office and later an antique store but now stands empty, revealing its age and structural infirmities.

"The last to fall were the buildings, distant and solemn, the gravestones for an entire world," wrote American author Dan Wells in his book *Partials*.

The unyielding passage of time eventually wearies all, but a building in Lohman continues to embody the entrepreneurial spirit of the Blochberger family. Hearts once emboldened by opportunities live on through this historical structure, helping prevent individual legacies from falling into obscurity. *(Primary photograph courtesy of Gert Strobel.)*

Charles W. Lohman – *The Lohman Store*

Many communities have been titled out of respect for pioneering spirits and dreamers who incurred the risks associated with building a business. In rural Cole County, there remains the legacy of an individual who embraced an opportunity presented by the coming of the railroad and was rewarded by having his name attached to a small town. Born in St. Louis on December 1, 1848, Charles W. Lohman was the oldest of eight children—two of whom died in infancy. His father, Charles F. Lohman, a native of Prussia, moved his family to Jefferson City when his oldest son was quite young.

According to *The Illustrated Sketch Book and Directory of Jefferson City and Cole County* printed in 1900, Charles W. Lohman was "educated in the public schools of Jefferson City." The book continued, "He later attended the Bryant & Stratton Commercial College in St. Louis, from which he graduated in 1870 . . . [H]e took a position as clerk on the steamer 'Viola Bell' of which his father was the owner and which operated between St. Louis and the head-waters of the Missouri."

As young men, Charles W. Lohman and his brothers. learned much from their father, who engaged in several successful mercantile interests and was an organizer and director of First National Bank in Jefferson City.

Charles W. Lohman built this store on Front Street in the early 1880s in the town for which he became the namesake. The building was torn down in 1917.

The experiences he received working aboard his father's steamboat helped prepare him for future entrepreneurial endeavors. They were cut short when the ship sank in 1871. The following year, he purchased a mercantile business on the corner of Dunklin and Jefferson Streets in Jefferson City previously owned by William Herman Morlock.

A milestone event occurred on December 11, 1873, when the twenty-five-year-old Lohman married Elizabeth Steininger. She was the daughter of Capt. Jacob Steininger, a German immigrant and Union veteran of the Civil War who served as a postmaster for Jefferson City. The couple raised one son, who was named Charles F. in honor of Lohman's father.

The 1889 edition of *Godspeed History of Cole County* noted that Lohman and his new wife moved to the growing community of Stringtown in 1874, purchasing a general store from Edward Linsenbardt in addition to a large swath of timber-covered property.

"Stringtown received its name, due to the fact that along a stretch of road about four miles long, there were 12 families who built log houses about 1/6 mile apart, farmed the land around their homes, but made most of their money by conducting a business of some sort," wrote the late O.W. Soell, a Lohman-area businessman. He added, "This four-mile road was traveled by stagecoach by nearly all the folks that wanted to go from Jefferson City to Springfield."

Located about two miles west of the North Moreau River in the center of Stringtown, Charles W. Lohman was appointed the town's postmaster in 1875, operating the post office from his store. Stringtown, in addition to serving as a stagecoach stop, boasted several businesses such as a dance hall, saloon, blacksmith, wagon-making shop, and a one-room log school.

Godspeed's History of Cole County explained that "in 1882, [Lohman] built a storehouse on the branch railroad recently completed through Cole County, and established a station there . . ." (This new store was located a couple miles north of his first store in Stringtown.)

A Lohman historical booklet printed in 1976 reveals that "the village of Lohman saw its establishment in 1882, continuing to be known by the familiar name of Stringtown. Exactly when the town began to be known as Lohman after its founder is not clear."

Records show that when the town was originally platted on February 11, 1882, it was recorded under the name of Stringtown, prior to becoming known as Lohman.

"Lohman's store did grow and prosper and soon a village began to build up below St. Paul's [Lutheran] Church and the storehouse and post office established by Charles W. Lohman," the Lohman historical booklet explained.

As a Lutheran and son of German immigrants, Lohman shared a connection with many area residents. As early as the 1830s, German immigrants began settling in the vicinity and, in 1852, organized St. Paul's Lutheran Church on a hill south of where Lohman's store was later established. Initially, Lohman opened his new store in partnership with John Henry Kautsch, naming the firm Lohman & Company. The Lohman historical booklet adds, "In 1885 Mr. Lohman moved his stock of goods from Stringtown to Lohman, and shortly after [1887] became sole possessor of the establishment."

On March 1, 1882, after the post office in Stringtown was closed, Lohman was commissioned as the first postmaster of the town that soon bore his name. Additionally, the forested property he owned in the Stringtown area began to be harvested and sold to the railroad for construction projects.

Little is known about Lohman's exit from the town other than he remained in business there until shortly after the turn of the century. On December 10, 1904, the fifty-six-year-old merchant died in Jefferson City. He was buried in Riverview Cemetery; his wife was laid to rest in 1932. His son, Charles F., was employed as a reporter in Spokane, Washington, when he died from a stroke in 1926; he was fifty-one years old.

The Lohman family has essentially disappeared from the area and the community carrying their name fell into decline when the railroad quit operating in 1962. Improvements made to local highways along with residents opting to travel to Jefferson City for employment also contributed to its business and population decrease.

An old adage asserts that "time marches on." However, as mentioned in the Russellville sesquicentennial book from 1988, "Lohman is a town that has maintained among its residents a neighborly fellowship and community spirit," thus serving as a reminder of the early vision of its namesake. *(Photographs courtesy of Gert Strobel.)*

Bandelier Mine and Farm – St. Martin

Simon Bandelier was Swiss, an immigrant who, after coming to Missouri in 1866, established himself as a farmer and livestock dealer in the area that became St. Martin. His farm was situated on the main road that was once dirt and gravel, pre-dating U.S. Highway 50. Around the turn of the 20th century, his farm was a beehive of activity with lead and coal deposits discovered in the area and served as a recreational destination for workers building the new state capitol.

"Simon was my great-great-grandfather and he built the house—a log cabin—that still stands on our property," said Ron

Bandelier. "One of his sons was Albert, who operated a coal mine that is just a short distance north of our property," he added.

The late 1890s and early 1900s witnessed much activity in the area with enterprising individuals motivated by the possibility of buried mineral deposits. Albert Bandelier, seeking to capitalize on such an opportunity, purchased the mining rights for a piece of land owned by local farmer William P. Schmitz.

Albert Bandelier, far right, owned and leased 80 acres of property in the St. Martin area to operate a coal mine. His younger brother, Emanuel, is on the far left. Eventually, cave-ins led to the mine's closure prior to World War I. Prior to it being shut down, he shipped railcars of coal to St. Louis.

Ron Bandelier explained, "He operated a coal mine near where the westbound U.S. Highway 50 exit lane in St. Martin intersects with State Highway D. The coal from this mine was as good as any Pennsylvania coal and apparently you could light it with a match." He continued, "We have records that show Albert shipped one hundred train loads of coal from the depot in Elston to be sold in St. Louis. I think it's pretty amazing that so much coal came out of that nearby mine."

Historical records maintained by Bandelier explain that a cave-in occurred and shut the mine down, although the specific date is unknown. Sometime later, Albert Bandelier sought to re-open the mine, but another cave-in occurred and it was abandoned.

"According to my father, Theodore, the mine had an elevator to access the mine shaft from which the workers hauled out the loads of coal using donkeys and carts," Bandelier said. "My father was about seven when he went down into the mine with his Uncle Albert and at that time the mine was closed, which was about 1912."

An annual report from the Missouri Division of Mines from 1913 notes that Bandelier's coal mine, listed as being located in Elston since St. Martin was not yet established, was one of only two noted coal mines in Cole County. The mine was covered and filled during the construction of the relocated Highway 50, which has since become Business 50.

"The cave-ins ended his mining operation but there were other mines that continued nearby," Ron Bandelier said. "There was one where the owners of the property managed to fool wealthy people from out east into investing in the mine by salting it, making it look like it was full of deposits."

Decades ago, when crews were expanding U.S. Highway 50 into four lanes, Theodore Bandelier told some of the bulldozer operators to be careful because there were still hidden shafts under the ground. One of the bulldozers later fell into a shaft when the earth gave way,

Beginning in 1913, Fairview Stock Farm in St. Martin became a site visited on the weekends by the construction crews building the new Missouri capitol building.

requiring another bulldozer to extract it.

"Not too many years ago, a sinkhole formed near the overpass along Highway D just outside St. Martins because one of the mine shafts collapsed," said Ron Bandelier. "The highway department had to fill it with large rocks and you can still see where all the fill work was done."

Although Albert's aspirations to become wealthy from coal mining operations came to an unexpected conclusion, he found another opportunity to capitalize on his family's rural setting by providing a welcomed entertainment venue.

On February 5, 1911, the second state capitol in Jefferson City was destroyed by fire after lightning struck the dome. Construction of the current capitol building began in 1913, bringing to Mid-Missouri scores of workers in the building industries.

"The structure will require several years to finish, as it is not only an imposing, but a massive, piece of architecture," reported the *Pleasant Hill Times* on March 20, 1914.

While they were building the new capitol, many of the workers came to visit the Bandelier place on the weekends, which was at the time known as Fairview Stock Farm.

"Albert and some of the family made wine and fermented it in the cellar of the log house so that they had it to sell to the workers," said Bandelier.

Anecdotal accounts passed down by Bandelier's father, Theodore, note that his Uncle Albert was arrested years later, during Prohibition, for making and selling wine, but his attorney was able to have him acquitted since the evidence had been "consumed." The completion of the capitol in 1917 brought an end to the workers' visits to the Bandelier place. As the years passed, Albert Bandelier remained involved in raising livestock and was ninety-five years old when he passed away in 1955.

"My father is now gone but he was able to share many of the stories of what happened on the farm so many decades ago, including the mining activities," said Ron Bandelier. "There's not a lot of information that has been written down about this and I always enjoyed hearing the stories from the family." He continued, "It's fascinating that there was such an active and productive mine nearby, which many people nowadays never knew existed. And the historic connection our farm had to the workers who helped build the Missouri Capitol is a piece of local history that I hope is remembered for generations to come." *(Photographs courtesy of Ron Bandelier.)*

Kiral's Brazito Garage - Brazito

An ambitious Carl "Bud" Norfleet erected a garage and service station in Brazito in 1928, becoming one of several successful and well-known commercial activities woven into the fabric of the community. In the years that followed, he witnessed several businesses come and go, but his original garage still stands and remains a fixture along U.S. Highway 54 south of Jefferson City.

For several decades, Norfleet ran his garage after building the original section consisting of a concrete block building and an awning covering gas pumps. In 1936, he built onto the building and later erected a small stand-alone structure to house a fuel truck and tanks for the storage of petroleum products. A garage section was added to the side of the building in 1946.

"Norfleet was basically the gas distributor for the area for several years," recalled Alan Kiral Sr. "Years earlier, on the north side of the garage, you could see parts of the old Arnhold General Store and hotel, but it's all long gone." He added, "When he built the garage, Highway 54 was a single-lane gravel road."

The business was operated by Norfleet for a quarter century, a period that included his service as an officer in the Ordnance Corps of the U.S. Army during World War II. In later years, he was employed by state government but leased the garage in Brazito for others to run.

The former Kiral's Brazito Garage is located along U.S. Route 54 in Brazito. The original section of the building was constructed by Charles Norfleet in 1928 and continues to serve the local community as a convenience store.

"I met Norfleet through a local farmer and decided to purchase the garage in 1968," said Kiral. "It took us a while to settle on the price but I bought it for $15,000 and he agreed to finance it at six percent interest. Sy Scruggs was operating the garage at the time and I paid $600 for his tools and inventory."

Kiral noted that in addition to the adjacent hotel and general store, there had also once been a walk-in icebox on the property. During the winter months, ice was cut from the local creeks and stored in sawdust inside the icebox for use in the warmer months.

"When I bought the business and some of the surrounding property," Kiral recalled, "Norfleet told me that they had put some silver coins and old newspapers in the northeast column of the canopy when they built the garage; it was a time capsule of sorts. Also,

Highway 54 was a two-lane paved highway when I started running it."

The *Sunday News and Tribune* printed in their April 27, 1969, edition, "Closer to Jefferson City, the dual laning of U.S. Route 54 from the Moreau River to Route D has been completed and construction is underway on a two-mile section between Route D and Route E near Brazito."

Kiral recalled, "During the time they were expanding Highway 54 into a four-lane, I was one of the only service stations open between Jefferson City and Eldon. I would have cars lined up and waiting for the gas pumps in the mornings and evenings."

Calling the business "Kiral's Brazito Garage," he not only performed repairs and maintenance on a wide range of automobiles but sold items including automotive products, groceries, liquor, tobacco, bait, and tackle along with hunting and fishing licenses. He was eventually approached by Tom Frasher, a local man who had

For five years, Kiral's Brazito Garage sponsored local racecar driver Tom Frasher, building him this 1969 Camaro.

gained some popularity for his abilities as a stock car driver. Frasher asked Kiral if he might consider becoming a sponsor of his racing events.

"I agreed and ended up sponsoring his racing for about five years," Kiral said. "The first year, I built him a 1955 Chevy, and his first night out, he came in third in both his races. He then told me what needed to be done to the car, I made the improvements and repairs, and the next week he came in second in both his races." He added, "After that, I made more improvements based upon his suggestions and he came in first in all his races the rest of the year. The following year, I build him a 1969 Camaro to run in his races and he won all kinds of trophies with that racecar."

Kiral continued to operate the vehicle repair and tow truck portion of the business for about twenty years before making the decision to transition to a full-retail convenience store. Shirley, his wife, assisted at the store and, for many years, performed the bookkeeping aspect of the business. Eventually, he erected a 30 x 62-foot addition on the south side of the main building in addition to another stand-alone structure on the north side. The latter was used for a number of business endeavors such as a laundromat, arcade room, restaurant, and even a "junk store."

Smiling, he recalled, "I installed three large red flags on top of the canopy and people driving down Highway 54 said they looked like they were glowing in the evening sun. When they asked me why I put three flags on the building, I always told them that Brazito wasn't big enough for six flags."

In 1999, after having operated the business for thirty-one years, Kiral retired and sold the store and property. Though now under different ownership, the former Kiral's Brazito Garage continues to serve the community as a convenience store and has become the community's only visible connection to its past businesses.

"There have been several important businesses in Brazito such as the old Arnhold General Store and the hotel, but they are all long gone," Kiral said. "But the original Norfleet Garage—the concrete block building and the canopy—are still there as part of the current convenience store." He concluded, "I was only a brief part of that history, but it's still nice to hear some of the folks around here still refer to it as Kiral's Store." *(Photographs courtesy of Alan Kiral Sr.)*

Arthur Jungmeyer – *Building contractor from Lohman/Russellville*

Born in 1906 on a farm in rural Cole County, Arthur Jungmeyer came from a pioneering family of German immigrants who helped establish St. Paul's Lutheran Church in Lohman. In his early years, he attended classes at both Lohman School and the German school at St. Paul's before eventually settling in a nearby community, where he would help contribute to the economic growth.

"In 1908, Dad [Wilhelm] bought the lumber yard in Lohman, sold it in 1912, and moved to a farm near Russellville," Arthur Jungmeyer explained several decades ago in handwritten notes. He added, "[I] started at Van Pool School District in 1912, and in the fall of 1918, moved on the farm near Lohman where my great grandpa from Germany settled in 1836."

An article appearing in a newsletter from Villa Marie (the nursing facility where Jungmeyer would later reside) noted, "At age 14, [Arthur] was recognized by the Bagnell Branch [Missouri Pacific Railroad] for extinguishing a fire on a railroad bridge close to the family farm. He was awarded $5.00 from the Railroad Company, which in 1920 was a handsome reward."

Aside from working on his family's farm, the next major step in Jungmeyer's employment came when he was hired at the Lohman Producer's Exchange in 1923, when only seventeen years old. Soon, he met the woman with whom he would spend the next several decades.

"He was married in 1928 to Ruth Goldammer," wrote the late L.A.B. Leslie in an article printed in the early 1970s. "They have two sons and two daughters," he added.

The book printed in 1988 for Russellville's sesquicentennial celebration stated, "In September 1929, the Board of Directors for the MFA Oil Company authorized the purchase of Standard Oil at Russellville for $200. The bulk plant, one of the original 25 of MFA Oil, opened for business in January 1930, with Arthur Jungmeyer as manager."

For nearly the next decade, Jungmeyer remained employed with MFA Oil as a wholesale distributor, making deliveries of assorted petroleum products throughout the area. The following years were an assortment of employment opportunities for Jungmeyer—he went to work for the MFA Exchange, the Jefferson City Baking Company, and finally entered the building trades. During World War II, he worked on construction projects at locations including Fort Leonard Wood and Scott Field, Illinois.

After the war, Jungmeyer fulfilled the role of city marshal for the community of Russellville. In 1947, city records reveal that he ticketed a local resident for "drinking and swearing." The defendant appeared before the town board and, for his violation, was fined $7.50.

Leveraging the training he received while working on government construction projects, "In 1952, he began his own business as a building contractor, building ninety-seven homes and various

other buildings in Jefferson City, Russellville, and throughout the surrounding areas," explained his obituary. One of the highlights of his contracting work included the development of the "Jungmeyer Addition," a community of homes he built west of the Russellville City Park and elementary school. His obituary added, ". . . [He] was a strong supporter of growth and betterment of the community."

His community-mindedness was not only represented by his commercial endeavors but by his participation in other volunteer activities around Russellville. Jungmeyer and his family were active mem-

Arthur Jungmeyer became a well-known construction contractor in the Russellville area and was recognized for being involved in the growth of the community of Russellville. In 1928, he married the former Ruth Goldammer at St. Paul's Lutheran Church in Lohman.

bers of Trinity Lutheran Church, serving on different boards and committees.

In addition to serving as an alderman with the city council of Russellville, he was also instrumental in the founding of the Russellville Lions Club, becoming a charter member on November 22, 1949. For decades, he supported the club as they sponsored many community improvements such as the development of the local water works and the volunteer fire department.

Charles W. Lohman built this store on Front Street in the early 1880s in the town for which he became the namesake. The building was torn down in 1917.

"Arthur Jungmeyer, a local contractor, has purchased the building which housed the Schubert Mercantile Company," reported the *California Democrat* on February 22, 1962. "He plans to repair and remodel the building."

The building, which dates back to the late 1890s, was soon remodeled and later held the offices of an insurance company, a local physician, and different stores. In December 1984, one of his sons, Don, opened Jungmeyer's Grocery in the former mercantile building. Another of Jungmeyer's four children, Marvin, engaged in his own business endeavors, operating for several decades the Jungmeyer Lumber Company in Russellville.

Jungmeyer is pictured in the early 1930s with the truck he used for making bulk petroleum deliveries for MFA Oil Company in Russellville.

Ever the visionary and constantly seeking ways to improve his community, Jungmeyer served on the board of the Russellville Senior Housing Association. The outcome of this effort was the construction of sixteen units of affordable senior housing located on a five-acre tract on the east side of town.

"Ruth had a severe stroke [on] September 25th, 1992, and died October 23rd, 1992," Jungmeyer wrote of his wife in later years. "We were married 64 years on that day. How we miss her every day."

Following the death of his beloved wife, he continued living in Russellville until age and infirmity necessitated his move to an assisted living facility. Frequently stating his desire to live to be one hundred years old, he passed away on May 6, 2006, just two months prior to achieving this goal. He was laid to rest alongside his wife in the Trinity Lutheran Church Cemetery near Russellville.

During his life, the impact he made on his community was recognized and appreciated by local residents. As the late L.A.B. Leslie, a fellow citizen of Russellville explained in an article in the 1970s, Arthur Jungmeyer deserved much of the credit for positive growth taking place in the town.

"He has been active in every worthwhile project in the community, giving generously of his time and money," Leslie wrote. "If it has anything to do with Russellville, we know that we can count on Art." *(Photographs courtesy of Jim and Eve Campbell.)*

Clarence O. Putnam – *Putnam Chevrolet in California*

Clarence O. "C.O." Putnam was a visionary of his time, seeking to build a business through an agreement with a vehicle manufacturing company that was little more than a decade old. What emerged from his efforts was a Chevrolet dealership that achieved the ripe age of one hundred years in 2023, at the time making it one of the oldest dealerships operating in the state of Missouri.

Born in 1897 in Cooper County, C.O. Putnam's father died as a young man; C.O. and his three siblings were then raised by their mother near Jamestown in Moniteau County. After graduating from the local high school, C.O. was working on a farm near the community of Lupus when World War I mandated his service to the nation.

C.O. Putnam, left, is pictured with his son, Donald, in the late 1970s. C.O. Putnam entered the automobile service business in 1923 after he was severely injured in a farming accident. His business, Putnam Chevrolet, celebrated its 100th anniversary in 2023 under the ownership of Bill Campbell.

Military records indicate the twenty-one-year-old was inducted into the U.S. Navy in St. Louis on July 13, 1918, and received his initial training in Great Lakes, Illinois. From there, he was sent to Norfolk, Virginia, prior to his brief assignment aboard the *USS Wisconsin*, a training ship moored at Philadelphia, Pennsylvania. It was during his assignment aboard this vessel that Putnam learned the duties of a fireman third class.

However, the war came to an end less than two weeks after he was assigned to the USS Wisconsin and, by January 23, 1919, he was on a passenger train and headed back home to Moniteau County.

"After he returned [from the military], we were married in September 1919," wrote his wife, the former Mildred Hoback, in a short biography for the *Moniteau County, Missouri Family History Book* printed in 1980. The two had met while attending high school together, she further explained.

Mildred continued, "We settled down to be farmers, but fate changed our lifestyle. C.O. broke his arm in such a way that he was left handicapped. We went into automobile service in Jamestown . . . in 1923," she added.

Known at the time as Putnam Motor Service, it was not until 1928 that C.O. Putnam secured a dealership with Chevrolet. He operated this business successfully for many years before entering a business relationship with another former farmer to purchase the Chevrolet dealership in Tipton, aptly naming it the Putnam-Gabert Chevrolet Company.

"TO THE PUBLIC," read the headline of an article in the *Tipton Times* on October 22, 1937. "Having purchased the Motor-Inn Garage and having been appointed Chevrolet dealers for this terri-

C.O. Putnam operated Putnam Motor Service in Jamestown for many years before expanding his dealership through partnerships in Tipton and California.

tory, we will be pleased to welcome old as well as new patrons."

Years later, an article printed in the *Tipton Times* on September 5, 1958, noted the Tipton dealership, "Mr. Putnam and Mr. [Paul]

Gabert started operating the business on October 18, 1937, as a partnership with Mr. Gabert as manager." The newspaper added, "Mr. Gabert, Clarence Putnam, and Joe Putnam [C.O.s younger brother] in partnership purchased the Chevrolet agency [Tompkins Chevrolet] in California in 1939."

By the mid-1940s, there were three dealerships carrying the Putnam name in whole or in part: Putnam-Gabert Chevrolet Company in Tipton, Putnam-Geiger Chevrolet Company in Jamestown, and Putnam Chevrolet in California. Putnam's success came in part by recognizing the sales successes of his employees. He hired Karl Herfurth at his dealership in 1931 and, by 1939, he had sold 100 automobiles. This achievement earned Herfurth the award of a $115 Hamilton watch in 1939.

In 1945, a modern brick dealership building was constructed on what was then U.S. Highway 50 in California. As the years came and went, C.O. Putnam's previous partnerships dissolved until such time as he only retained the dealership in California.

"Our two children, Norma and Don, graduated from Jamestown High School and [the] University of Missouri," wrote Mildred Putnam in 1980. "Norma died in 1961, age 41. Don has worked 27 years for Sperry Gyroscope and General Dynamics. Don, his wife, Fran, and two children are now living in California . . ., where he is General Manager of Putnam Chevrolet."

Don Putnam, who had served as a junior officer with the U.S. Army in the Korean War, later worked for companies that supported the early Mercury and Apollo missions. In 1980, while on leave from General Dynamics, he took over his father's Chevrolet dealership and ran the company for the next three years.

"I began working for C.O. Putnam as a technician in 1977 and became parts manager under Don Putnam in 1981," explained Bill Campbell, current owner of Putnam Chevrolet. "In 1983, I became service manager, and then from 1983 to 2018, Don Putnam and I were partners in the company."

With the rerouting of U.S. Highway 50 south of California, the decision was made to relocate the dealership along the northwest junction of State Highway 87 and the new U.S. Highway 50 in 2014. In 2018, Bill Campbell assumed primary ownership of Putnam Chevrolet while his son-in-law, Adam Weber, became a minority partner.

"Adam's great-grandfather Earl Eberhardt owned Eberhardt Chevrolet in California during the same time that C.O. Putnam had his dealership in Jamestown," Campbell said. "What very interesting historical connections!"

The company's namesake, C.O. Putnam, was eighty-five years old when he passed away in 1982; he is interred in the California Masonic Cemetery. His son, Donald, died in 2020 and is buried in the Columbia Cemetery.

The history of Putnam Chevrolet is highlighted by its achievement of reaching the century mark, which Bill Campbell noted is an impressive milestone for an automobile dealership and serves as a testament to the vision of its founder, C.O. Putnam.

The extensive legacy of Putnam Chevrolet came to a close on February 6, 2023, when it was sold to the Ed Morse Automotive Group of Delray Beach, Florida. *(Photographs courtesy of Bill Campbell.)*

Lohman, Mo., _____ 191_

German Mutual Windstorm and Tornado Insurance Association
Lohman, Cole County, Mo.

Received of _____

Initiation fees (20 cents per $100.00) .... $_____
Assessment No.____ .... $_____
Total _____ $_____

_____ Appraiser, Treasurer

German Mutual Insurance Company – *Lohman*

Inspired by a cooperative spirit and demonstrating a streak of self-reliance, a group overwhelmingly consisting of German Lutherans gathered at the parochial schoolhouse at St. Paul's Lutheran Church in Lohman on September 5, 1891. It was on this date that they set about organizing a company to provide for the insurance needs of their friends and family who were operating farms in Cole County.

"The history of farm mutuals dates back to the late 1800s because there was not any insurance for the farmers, so they formed their own organization," said Glen Steenbergen, president of the board of the German Mutual Insurance Company.

Known as the Farmers Fire and Lightning Insurance Company, Andy Knernschield was elected as temporary chairman along with board members Peter Reisdorff, Ed Baumann, Andy Hoffman, J.F. Hiittenmeyer, Gus Fischer, John Doehla, and Mat Gratz. George Fikenscher, who was at the time serving as pastor of St. Paul's, was elected as the board's first secretary.

Rev. Fikenscher holds the distinction as the longest-serving pastor of St. Paul's Lutheran Church, beginning with his installation in August 1875 and ending with his retirement in December 1904. In addition to his association with the insurance mutual, he was active in the community and became an original trustee when Lohman was incorporated in 1910.

"In 1901, the name of the company was changed to the German Fire Insurance Association," explained the Russellville sesquicentennial book printed in 1988.

The company quickly gained solvency and on November 17, 1905, the *Russellville Rustler* reported that they had 400 members and

George Fikenscher is pictured with a group of students outside the former parish schoolhouse at St. Paul's Lutheran Church in Lohman. It was inside this schoolhouse in 1891 that the organization that became the German Mutual Insurance Company was established, with Fikenscher serving as the first board secretary.

possessed an insured value of $602,260.

The Russellville sesquicentennial book added, "After suffering many windstorm losses, the members of the first insurance company organized the Windstorm Insurance Company on January 28, 1918."

For the first ten years, Rev. George Fikenscher continued to serve as the secretary. He was succeeded by Henry Raithel, who served for the next thirty-five years, and was followed by August Doehla, who fulfilled the role until his death in 1969. Those later serving as secretaries for the company were Lenora Doehla, Alfred Ehrhardt, Stephen Coffelt, Glen Steenbergen, and, most recently, Candace Stockton.

"The insurance policies have always been through word of mouth," said Edgar Kautsch, a long-time agent for the company. "My grandparents, John and Amelia Kautsch, and my father, Gus, were all insured through the company." Edgar Kautsch continued,

"We insure houses, barns, machinery, contents . . . almost anything without licenses such as vehicles and trailers. Although we used to write policies only in Cole County, we can now write them anywhere in the state of Missouri."

Like many insurance mutuals seeking to maintain competitive rates, there have been instances in the company's history when the board was hesitant to pay claims of questionable nature or those that appeared to fall outside the purview of the written policy coverage.

"A jury yesterday awarded $200 to Marion O. Huff, plaintiff in a suit against German Mutual Fire Insurance

John Kautsch, grandfather of current German Mutual agent Edgar Kautsch, had coverage through the Lohman area farm mutual in the 1930s.

Association on an insurance policy covering a team of mules," printed the *Daily Capital News* on March 9, 1943. "Huff alleges in his suit that he insured two mules against loss by fire or lightning and that the team had been killed by a bolt of lightning during a storm," the newspaper added. "Huff had asked for $300 for his team and costs."

Another significant change in the structure of the company occurred on May 28, 1974. During a special meeting, the decision was made to merge the German Mutual Fire Insurance Association and the Windstorm Insurance Company to form what is presently known as the German Mutual Insurance Company.

"The board will generally meet four times a year at the Lohman Community Building, although occasionally there might be a special meeting held," shared Edgar Kautsch.

Since the company's inception, there have been several who have served as board president, such as Andreas Knernschield, Peter Reisdorff, Theodore Raithel, and Anton Heidbreder.

Glen Steenbergen recalled, "I had an insurance agent's license and when Anton Heidbreder died in 2006, I took over for him. I was an agent, secretary, and board member for several years before becoming the board president."

For forty-five years, Lohman native Cletus Heidbreder conducted the duties of treasurer for the company. Since his passing in 2015, his wife, Ethel, has served in this capacity.

"At this point, we have more than 430 insured members," said Edgar Kautsch. "As I said before, we really don't do any advertising other than having a history of referrals through word of mouth."

Glen Steenbergen explained that although the company may not have the size and resources of industry insurance giants, it remains strong and continues to provide the vital service for which it was initially established more than a century ago.

"The German Lutherans around Lohman were always very independent, and they found a way to take care of their insurance needs by forming what is now the German Mutual Insurance Company," Steenbergen said. "We may not be among the largest of companies, but we remain solvent and have survived in a time when many other companies have merged." He concluded, "Many of the descendants of those original German Lutherans who formed the company still live in the area and serve on our board. They are a very financially conservative people who work hard to take care of what they have." *(Photographs courtesy of Edgar Kautsch.)*

The Scrivner Store – Scrivner

The town of Scrivner, located a few miles southeast of Russellville, is now little more than a scattering of buildings along a stretch of country road. But for years, it was a well-known destination because of a small general store that provided a range of necessities and other unique items for area residents. John Enoch Scrivner became the namesake for the small community after building a two-story home around 1884. He initially engaged in mercantile endeavors from his home but then erected a store building across the road in 1889, providing additional space for his increasing line of products.

Thomas A. Miles is pictured with his granddaughter, Brenda Crain, around 1950-1951. They are sitting on the porch of the Scrivner Store south of Russellville, which has been used as a residence for the last several decades.

"Next, he added a blacksmith shop across the road," explained an article featured in the souvenir booklet printed for Russellville's sesquicentennial in 1988. The booklet added, "Merchandise for the store was shipped by rail to Russellville, or Mr. Scrivner went to Jefferson City and brought back a wagon load of items."

Doris Scrivner Collier noted in her detailed genealogy work, *The Descendants of Benjamin Scrivner,* that John Scrivner placed a post office in the back of the store in 1896 and received an appointment as the postmaster for the community by President Grover Cleveland.

In her book *The Ghost Towns of Central Missouri,* Kelly Warman-Stallings wrote, "Prior to the turn of the century, the store caught fire on two separate occasions. The first time it burned partially; the second time it burned completely. The third store was rebuilt around 1900."

The book mentions that there was a steel safe that John Scrivner had installed in the store, which reportedly crashed through the floor both times the building burned.

John Scrivner and some of his family eventually chose to move their mercantile interests to Oklahoma, selling the Scrivner Store to Obediah Marcus "Mark" Lovell. A few years earlier, in 1896, Lovell had built a blacksmith shop in Scrivner. He was married to Dollie, the daughter of Nehemiah Scrivner and a relative of John Scrivner.

Lovell continued to operate the general store for several years with the assistance of his wife. However, in 1913, they sold the business and moved to Enon, living on a nearby farm and operating a general store in the community. The Scrivner Store was purchased by Thomas Miles, who was married to Lucinda Scrivner, another of Nehemiah's daughters.

Brenda Crain, granddaughter of Thomas Miles explained, "The blacksmith shop burned down, and around 1917 they built the Scrivner Church of Christ near the store. Also," she added, "during the transition from horse and buggies to automobiles, gas pumps were installed in front of the store."

Thomas Miles' wife passed away in 1946 and

This steel safe fell through the floor both times the Scrivner Store burned. It has been passed down to a descendant of the store's founder, John Scrivner. Courtesy of Andrew Seaver

Crain recalls that her grandfather, who had been living in the two-story house across the street built by John Scrivner, decided to move into the store building.

"My parents then moved into the house and my grandfather continued to operate the store," she said. "I have so many good memories of sitting on the front steps with him and he would give me candy from some of the containers."

Her older brother, the late Freddie Miles, wrote a few reflections about the store in the years prior to his passing. He explained that you could find "just about everything—coffee, sugar, trimmed plug tobacco with a butcher knife, wild game, material, jewelry, shoes ($2.00 a pair), dishes, clothing, and hardware."

Crain recalls that her grandfather ran the store until shortly before he died in 1953. After his death, her parents purchased the store and began the process of remodeling, adding a room on one side of the structure. Eventually, they moved out of the two-story home across the road and into the store.

"Before the remodel happened, the store was just one long room," Crain said. "At that time, it did not have an indoor bathroom but rather an outhouse that was behind the building."

Plumbing and a restroom were eventually installed and Crain recalls that for a couple of years, while she and her parents lived in the former Scrivner Store, the Clark Township elections were held in their living room.

"There wasn't a lot of room and the election judges had a table and there were a couple of voting booths," Crain recalled. "Mom would make the election judges a big meal and at the end of the day they put all of the ballots in a gunny sack, sealed the top with some type of wax ring, and then took it to Jefferson City."

Years later, when her parents passed away, her brother, Freddie Miles, moved into the store and did some additional remodeling, adding a second room. After his death, Crain and her husband lived in the old store for a year while they built a home south of Russellville. The Scrivner Store continues to serve as a home for members of the Crain family, maintaining a connection to its creator, John Scrivner. The old safe that miraculously survived two fires and years of use, is now in the home of one of Thomas Miles' great-grandsons.

"I can clearly recall all of the times going to that store as a kid and my grandfather spoiling me by giving me all the candy that I wanted," Crain smiled. "I spent a lot of time with him there and that was a good place to be as a child." In warm reflection, she added, "That old store will probably outlive me and I hope that it stays in the family for a long time to come." *(Courtesy of Brenda Crain.)*

CHAPTER 5

Faith

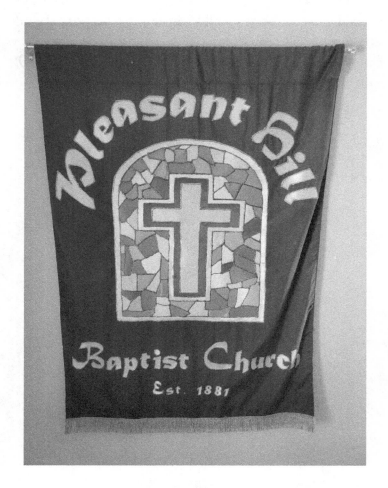

Pleasant Hill Baptist Church – Brazito area

Churches have oftentimes been described using the symbolism of a large family. Many congregations tend to grow throughout the years and watch as their offspring move on to begin building their own families, or, as this metaphor might suggest, leaving their home churches to form new congregations in other locations. Pleasant Hill Baptist Church, located on Heritage Highway near Brazito, represents one such church family. It came into existence through the efforts of a dedicated missionary pastor, a small group of Christian faithful, and the help of a well-established church in the area.

"On the 22nd day of October 1881, [Baptist] Brothers Wilson Allee, E.W. Lumpkin, and R.A. Stark met with a number of God's people at the Pleasant Hill School House for the purpose of con-

Pleasant Hill Baptist Church was organized in the Pleasant Hill School House north of Brazito in 1881. The first church was located at the junction of Scriver Road and State Route D but was moved in the 1950s to its current location on Heritage Highway.

stituting them into a church," noted the *Consitution, By-Laws, and Historical Sketch of the Pleasant Hill Baptist Church* printed in 1977.

Remnants of the Pleasant Hill School House, which was sold in 1952, remain on State Highway D. During one of the follow-up meetings held at the school, plans for a church building materialized and a congregation came into being under the guidance of Cole Spring Baptist Church near Russellville.

"My mother, who is in her 90s, used to attend the Pleasant Hill School when she was a child and has pointed out its location many times," said Kim Smith, a Baptist pastor who was a member of Pleasant Hill Baptist Church for more than three decades.

"By motion and second they agreed to build a church house and . . . [a] . . . committee was appointed to secure a location . . ." the aforementioned booklet added. "The building was to be 26 feet wide and 40 feet long, and a frame building was planned with three rows of seats with two aisles, and two doors . . . in one end."

The first church building was erected on property donated by congregation member Jim Glover and located on the south side of the junction of Scrivner Road and State Highway D. Edward M. Lumpkin was selected to serve as the first pastor for the new Pleasant Hill Baptist Church.

E.M. Lumpkin became a well-known missionary pastor throughout Mid-Missouri and did not remain long at the fledgling church. He went on to pastor at churches in locations such as Hickory Hill and Spring Garden, also helping to establish congregations in communities that included Corticelli and Ulman. Two years after this initial meeting, in 1883, the Pleasant Hill Cemetery was estab-

A parsonage was dedicated next to the current church in January 1964. It is now used in support of a variety of church functions.

lished on nearby Bainer Road. For many years, the church maintained an association with the cemetery and assisted in its upkeep.

"I can remember when I was a kid, there were several of us from the church who helped clean up the cemetery on occasion," Kim Smith recalled.

Sunday school was established in 1896 and the church welcomed several pastors throughout the intervening years, most of whom shared their pastoral services with other congregations since worship was not held every Sunday in the early decades of the church.

"Rev. Walter Connor of Jefferson City held services at the Pleasant Hill Baptist Church Sunday, December 20th," reported the *Jefferson City Post-Tribune* on January 3, 1930. "Reverend Connor has been chosen to be the pastor of this church during 1930."

The church building was later updated with gas lamps and underwent remodeling. The building became a fixture of the small Pleasant Hill community and was used to host ice cream socials and revivals. In the mid-1940s, a well was drilled to supply water and, in 1948, electricity was installed. Blessed with increasing membership, there unfolded discussions regarding the construction of a larger church. Rev. Farrie Cole Jr., a respected local pastor, led the church through many of these discussions. In 1953, Pleasant Hill began holding full-time worship services, but Rev. Cole accepted the call to become full-time pastor for Mt. Olive Baptist Church.

"In November 1955, it was decided by ballot to build the church on Highway 54," explained the church history. "Anna Manning graciously offered to give part of her land for the new building."

Lumber for the new church came from timber donated by the congregation and they moved into their new building on December 14, 1957. Church records confirm that the old church building was sold to help pay off debts associated with the new construction. A parsonage was built next to the church and dedicated in January 1964. The next year, a wooden steeple was added to the front of the church and has been rebuilt using synthetic materials. U.S. Highway 54 moved in the early 1970s when expanding into four lanes and the front of the church now faces Heritage Highway. Additionally, the previous church building has been demolished.

"My wife and I married in 1964 and moved to a farm in the [Brazito] area the next year," said Mel Callahan. "I taught Sunday school at Pleasant Hill for many years and participated in the church's successful bus ministry."

Callahan, who received his license to preach at Pleasant Hill, now ministers at a Baptist church in St. Elizabeth. However, he recognizes that the congregation at Pleasant Hill remains dedicated to the scriptures and embraces opportunities to outreach in the surrounding areas.

"The church is very diverse in its membership—some work in town, some live on a farm," he said. "There are those who are financially well off and others who may be below the poverty level." He added, "Churches are like people in that they have unique personalities. At Pleasant Hill Baptist Church, the personality is one that is friendly and outgoing, where you can always find someone with whom you can relate." *(Photographs courtesy of Jeremy P. Ämick.)*

Hickory Hill Baptist Church – *Hickory Hill*

Several townships in Cole County have a deep and abiding connection to houses of worship. These churches often weathered unique storms and have occasionally outlived the communities in which they were established. Such is the case with the once-thriving settlement in the southwestern section of the county where little remains but a vibrant Baptist congregation.

"The story of Hickory Hill Baptist Church began with seven faithful Christians deciding to hold an unsuspecting meeting," explained a booklet printed for the church's sesquicentennial celebration in 2010. The booklet added, "William Johnston, William Barr, James M. Ballinger, Elizabeth Johnston, Matilda Ballinger, Sally Bond, and Isabella Russell first met in the Sullens schoolroom at Iduma College in Cole County on Saturday, October 27, 1860. The purpose of that meeting was to organize a Baptist church upon the principles of the Concord Association of . . . Missouri."

Established in 1860, Hickory Hill Baptist Church moved from their location in Bethel Cemetery next to the cemetery in Hickory Hill, where they built this church building in 1911. The church has undergone many expansions throughout the years and remains one of the few surviving links to Hickory Hill's past.

Establishing a church covenant, this visionary group named their new congregation Iduma after the former college where they first gathered. The name later changed to Ebenezer Baptist Church when they erected a church building in a grove of trees in an area now identified as Bethel Cemetery near Hickory Hill.

"Hickory Hill, fourteen miles southwest of Jefferson City, was platted by M.H. Belshe for John Lumpkin in 1867," wrote James E. Ford in *A History of Jefferson City, Missouri's State Capital, and of Cole County.*

The church began holding business meetings in 1878 and the following year sent its first delegates to the local Concord Baptist Association. In 1880, the first Sunday school superintendent was elected, and a decision was soon made about the future location of the church.

As the nearby town of Hickory Hill began to grow, so did the congregation of the church. In the *Illustrated Sketch Book and Directory of Jefferson City and Cole County* printed in 1900, it is noted that Hickory Hill boasted a population of seventy-five in addition to businesses that included merchants, a blacksmith, sawmills, a physician, livestock breeder, wagon maker, and post office.

According to the *Miller County Autogram-Sentinel* in its October 27, 1960, edition, the church "was later moved to the present site [in Hickory Hill] and [became] known as the Hickory Hill Baptist Church."

Church records indicate that following the move, the congregation shared a two-story building with Hickory Hill Lodge 211,

a Masonic fraternity. The building was situated along a gravel road that became Highway 54. Adjacent to the church building was Hickory Hill Cemetery—a community cemetery with a burial marker dating to

The church was once located along the then-gravel Highway 54. In the early 1970s, the highway moved a short distance to the west when it was expanded into four lanes.

1870.

"After the present structure was built in 1911 (just east of the old one) the latter was turned over to the Masons, moved to the village of Eugene, and is now the Lodge Hall and the Town Hall," explained a church historical bulletin. "The lot reverted to the . . . cemetery for a parking space."

By the fall of 1917, the finances of Hickory Hill Baptist Church had grown to the extent that they could raise the pastor's yearly salary to $250. Several weeks later, the first church budget was approved; prior to this, committees visited members at their homes to request donations for mission work and operating expenses.

Discipline was also an interesting facet of early church history since members caught engaging in undesired behaviors such as the use of profane language, running a saloon, or dancing, being excluded from membership in the church.

The stock market crash of 1929, which heralded the beginning of the Great Depression, also signaled a brief period of financial difficulties for the congregation. This resulted in a reduction in the number of worship services held and lowered the pastor's salary. Highway 54, stretching in front of the church, was paved in 1932. By 1935, the church appeared to be weathering the Great Depression through increased tithing and offerings.

"There were 24 additions to the church; 9 by letter and 15 by baptism," reported the *Word and Way* on November 7, 1935, in an article describing a recent "spirit-filled revival." The article continued, "Hickory Hill is fortunate to have a fine board of deacons, real prayer warriors for Christ."

The next several decades were expressed through growth, accompanied by the addition of a basement under the church building, construction of a new auditorium, remodeling of the old auditorium into an educational building, and erection of a parsonage. Additional acreage was later purchased for the church and in 2016 a new multi-purpose building was dedicated.

"Hickory Hill had been platted decades ago, and with all of the growth of the church, we had to make sure that we did not cover up any platted roads when we expanded," said Wilburn Hoskins, who has been a member of the congregation since 1951.

"When I was a child, we had a junior choir and sang in front of the church every Sunday," he recalled. "My father was licensed to preach at Hickory Hill in 1955 and he went on to preach at several small churches in the surrounding area while many of my family members were deacons," he added.

The original church site is home to Bethel Cemetery a short distance to the north. Highway 54 passed in front of the church but has since become United Road after construction of the four-lane highway in the early 1970s. Hickory Hill Baptist Church sits off the beaten path but is a bustling congregation dedicated to outreach and growth.

"The church has been a bigger part of my life and that of my family," said Hoskins. "The multi-purpose building has also been a blessing for our congregation. It brings children and their families together for events, where there are some who do not attend a church. It is here that we are able to share brief devotionals between games and activities." He concluded, "You never know who is listening when a devotion is shared and that allows us to share the church's mission and plant little seeds of faith." *(Photographs courtesy of Wilburn Hoskins.)*

Father Francis "Joseph" Reisdorff – *Stringtown*

Father Francis "Joseph" Reisdorff is interred in a historic Catholic cemetery near the North Moreau River on the eastern edge of Stringtown. For several decades, his burial site remained unmarked but has recently received renewed attention after it was discovered that the priest established several Catholic parishes in Texas and inspired German festivals that continue to this day. His story began in Prussia on October 4, 1840, when he was born the third of nine children of Peter Reisdorff and Theresia Angenendt. His parents immigrated to the United States the following year, eventually settling on a farm near Lohman. They were among a group of early immigrants who established the Catholic mission of St. Joseph near Stringtown.

"After coming to America, [Joseph Reisdorff] studied in St Francis Seminary, Milwaukee, Wisconsin, and was ordained March 16, 1872," explains records maintained by Holy Family Church in Nazareth, Texas.

Historical documents reveal that the priest spent the next twenty years working in the Archdiocese of St. Louis, which included leading Catholic parishes in the Missouri communities of Columbia, California, Cottleville, and Manchester.

Following his death, Father Reisdorff was interred next his parents in the Catholic cemetery in Stringtown. A new marker has recently been set to denote his burial site. Courtesy of Jeremy P. Amick

"Rev. Jos. Reisdorff, the popular pastor of the Catholic Church of this city for the past two years, has accepted a call to take charge of a church near St. Charles . . .," reported the *California Democrat* on November 23, 1876. "Mr. Reisdorff has, by his exemplary conduct and gentlemanly demeanor, won the confidence not only of his congregation, but of our entire community, and we regret very much his departure from our midst," the newspaper added.

But his ministry in Missouri came to an end in 1891, after he was advised by physicians that his health was suffering in Missouri climates. It was then he began to focus on building new Catholic parishes and settlements in Texas.

The fifty-one-year-old priest arrived in Windthorst, Texas, on December 31, 1891. He soon began advertising in Catholic and German newspapers throughout the Midwest, appealing to German immigrants to join the new settlement he was developing.

"Father Reisdorff served as a pastor to the new colony of Windthorst until March 1895," noted a historical booklet from Holy Family Church in Nazareth, Texas. "Why he left Windthorst is still a disputed question. When Father Reisdorff was preparing to leave Windthorst, that colony was still in the midst of an altercation with Clark and Plumb, the company from which the Windthorst colony lands had been purchased."

Seeking the best circumstances for settling new colonies, Father Reisdorff left in the midst of the financial quarreling to locate other opportunities for pioneering German families. This unyielding passion for establishing new settlements where they could live, work and worship carried him next to Rhineland (Texas), on March 19, 1895.

"The . . . roots of Rhineland and St. Joseph Catholic Church are permanently intertwined," reported the *Abilene Reporter-News* on September 2, 1995. "Both trace back to 1895 when a Catholic priest, the Rev. Joseph Reisdorff, and a land agent, Hugo Herchenbach, got together—the priest to establish a farming community for German Catholics who wanted to get away from the cities, and the agent to promote settlements and sell land."

In 1902, Father Reisdorff traveled to Nazareth, Texas, spending the next four years establishing the congregation known as Holy Family Church. In 1906, the colonizer traveled approximately thirty miles to Umbarger and helped found a new community along with St. Mary's Catholic Church.

His fifth and final legacy of colonizing Catholic communities came in 1911 when he "traveled to the developing railroad community of Slaton, where he continued to recruit German Catholics from the Midwest and German Lutherans from Central Texas," wrote Lee Williams for the Texas Highways website. Williams further explained, "Reisdorff served as the first priest at St. Joseph Catholic Church in Slaton, but he stayed occupied as a businessman and was paid a commission on land sold in the area to Catholic families."

Reisdorff fell ill beginning in 1917 and suspended his service as the parish priest. He continued living in Slaton and was eighty-one years old when he died on January 28, 1922. His remains, after being celebrated in a mass at St. Joseph Catholic Church (Texas), were transported to Missouri and interred alongside his parents in the St. Joseph Catholic Cemetery near Stringtown and Lohman.

The mission church of St. Joseph in Stringtown was closed in the early 1890s and little exists to denote its historic past other than an old stone foundation for the former church and a small cemetery. St. Michael Catholic Church in Russellville now maintains the cemetery in perpetuity.

Since helping establish five settlements across North Texas and the Panhandle of Texas decades ago, Reisdorff's influence continues to live on through German heritage festivals. The festivals, though not directly attributed to Reisdorff, provide an interesting connection between those communities in Texas and that of the St. Michael parish in Russellville.

"We have a festival at St. Michael every fall that features a lot of German-style foods such as sausages and sauerkraut," said Mike Kirchner. "It really feels as though it is a shared connection between the Texas parishes and ours."

Kirchner also noted that several years ago, they discovered that Father Reisdorff was buried in the old cemetery in Stringtown, but did not possess a grave marker. Through the coordination of Monsignor Robert Kurwicki and the dedication of members of St. Michael, a memorial marker was acquired and installed on the gravesite.

"Our parish is responsible for the cemetery and when we found out that there was a priest buried there without a marker, we wanted to make sure that was corrected," he affirmed. Kirchner added, "We all felt that it was our obligation to do so, and now that the marker is set, it will help ensure that Farther Reisdorff's contributions are not forgotten." (*Primary photograph courtesy of Holy Family Catholic Church, Nazareth, Texas.*)

Scrivner Church of Christ – Scrivner

Time has carried away memories of many small communities throughout Mid-Missouri, erasing evidence of bustling settlements built upon the dreams of foresighted men and women. Yet the near-forgotten Scrivner, a "bump in the road" near Russellville, maintains a connection to its distant past through a building known as the Scrivner Church of Christ.

"In the 1880s, John [Scrivner] built a house approximately seven miles southeast of Russellville . . .," wrote Doris Scrivner Collier in *The Descendants of Benjamin Scrivner*. She added, "The house was the first building in the town of Scrivner. John sold groceries from his house for a time and then built a general store."

The town's activity increased with the addition of a blacksmith shop and a post office, the latter of which operated out of the rear of Scrivner's store. It was, however, dissension at a nearby church that brought its own house of worship to the community.

"There was a congregation located near Brazito . . .," explained the souvenir book printed for Russellville's sesquicentennial in 1988. "This congregation split over the music question. Those who wanted [instrumental] music [during worship] went to the southwest, a short way from the former location, and built a building known as Mt. Union Christian Church [no longer there]."

Located along Scrivner Road south of Russellville, the Scrivner Church of Christ was for many years an important part of the community. Erected between 1917-1918, the congregation disbanded in 2010 and the building is now privately owned.

The book further notes that those not wanting instrumental music in worship went on to form Scrivner Church of Christ, built along Scrivner Road near the general store once owned by John Scrivner.

The spiritual foundation for the congregation was laid in 1914 when Reverend J.L. Davis—a Christian minister and noted scriptural debater from Kentucky—held a tent meeting in the (former)

Mt. Carmel Schoolhouse. This inspired local families to begin meeting for worship in local homes.

Three years later, in 1917, Rev. Davis returned to hold a tent meeting at Scrivner. It was during this event that these families resolved to erect a permanent house of worship in their community.

Established in 1884 by local merchant John Scrivner, the community of Scrivner is now little more than a scattered collection of homes and a former church building.

"The one-acre of land for the church was donated by Manuel Scrivner," said Brenda (Miles) Crain, who began attending the church with her parents in the years following her birth. She continued, "C.E. [Charles Edward] Stark was a carpenter who oversaw the construction of the church and also served as one of the first elders of the fledgling congregation. After the building was finished in 1918, his son, Archie Stark, served as the first minister of the Scrivner Church of Christ."

Prior to his death in 1981, Archie Stark, a U.S. Navy veteran of World War I, was employed for thirty-nine years by the Community Bank of Russellville.

In her book *The Ghost Towns of Central Missouri*, Kelly Warman-Stallings explained, "R.L. [Ray Leonidus] Gaither donated the trees from his land to be made into lumber so that the church could be built . . ."

In these early times, "The mode of travel to church was by horseback, muleback, farm wagon, surreys, and buggies," wrote the late Golda Ross, a long-time member of the congregation. For many years, the church remained relatively untouched by time, heated by a wood stove and lighted by gas lamps. But as the congregation began to grow, improvements were made to the original building. Ross also shared the names of some of the early congregation members: Enloe, Scrivner, Payne, Miles, Roark, Stark, Deuschle, Bond, Baysinger, Tyree, and Gaither.

"There have really been minimal changes to the church, but eventually they built classrooms and bathrooms in the back of the building," said Brenda Crain. "A well was also drilled for water and there was a small porch added to the front." Smiling, she added, "The old outhouse still stands behind the church building."

Crain also noted that the church was eventually updated with electricity in the early 1940s and Scrivner Road, which had originally been gravel, was paved by the county in 1995.

"Ferris Wall, who was from the Ulman area, used to come lead our services about every fourth or fifth Sunday," said Brenda Crain. "When we didn't have a preacher, Raymond or Cletus Payne would deliver a message from the pulpit."

Since the early 1970s, Tom Crain—husband to Brenda and a graduate of Freed-Hardeman University in Henderson, Tennessee— regularly delivered sermons at the small church. However, as older members of the congregation passed and younger ones moved on. Because of this and also its remote location, services were no longer sustainable.

"Our last service was in June of 2008," said Tom Crain, who also holds the distinction of being the church's last minister.

Brenda Crain said, "The property was eventually sold to [the late] Gail Wiser, whose family still owns the church building and property. A very special item we obtained was the original pulpit, from which my husband delivered many sermons during the years." She added, "I sat in front of that pulpit for many years and it really means a lot to me."

The church building is now being used for personal events such as family gatherings for the Wiser family.

The building that was for decades home to the congregation of Scrivner Church of Christ has become one of the few anchors to the community's past, while the store, blacksmith shop, and post office have all but faded into distant memory. Although the church no longer resonates with worship services, Crain maintains that she clings to a heart full of loving memories.

"Sometimes I like living in the past and that church represents a simpler time in my life," she said. "I made many wonderful, lifelong friends there." Pausing, she added, "Of course, many who attended there were biological family, but those who weren't, we considered them brothers and sisters in Christ." *(Photographs courtesy of Brenda Crain.)*

Enon Baptist Church – *Enon*

The community of Enon, near the southeast corner of Moniteau County, came into existence through the entrepreneurial spirit of James McGinnis, who built the first house in the developing community in 1869. In the coming years, the McGinnis family became involved in businesses and community activities—most notably a bank and a church. These two early structures remain one of few surviving links to his vision and a town that has nearly faded with the loss of mining operations and a railroad spur.

"The railroad coming through Enon in 1881 contributed to its growth," wrote the late Dorothy Medlen in a summary for the

1988 book celebrating the sesquicentennial of Russellville. "A plat was made in 1891 by Mr. McDowell and Mr. [Andrew] McGinnis and presented at the Moniteau County Courthouse," she added.

More than one popular story has been handed down through generations that explains how the settlement of Enon received its name. However, the most widely accepted has biblical roots that refer to a watery site named AEnon, where, it was written, John the Baptist performed baptisms.

This 1904 photograph features John Henry Jones, left, an early deacon of Enon Baptist Church. Next to him is John McGinnis, also an early church member who served as the first president of Enon Exchange Bank. Courtesy of Christopher Jones

"[Mary Jane] McGinnis gave the name AEnon to the village when the Post Office was established back in the [1880s]," noted the *Historical Sketch of the Concord Baptist Association and its Churches*, printed in 1973. "The name was taken from John 3:23 and seemed fitting because the Moreau River flowed through the community and often flooded the lowlands."

The railroad helped inspire several business endeavors such as a grist mill, general merchandise stores, a harness shop, a poultry house, and a drug store, to name but a few. One-room schoolhouses were also built in the area throughout the next several years and included New Zion School, Lincoln School, Mt. Herman School, and Contention School (later renamed Enon School).

Yet this slow and steady growth brought on by the railroad would soon be eclipsed by a massive, but short-lived, population explosion.

"Enon reached its peak as a boom town in 1901, when the mining town sprung up, on the hill west of town known as Tatesville," explained the 1980 book *Moniteau County, Missouri History*. The book added, "It was platted by N.O. Tate, who was a foreman for the Central Missouri Mining Company. Miners rushed in and the population soon reached 750."

An article appearing in the *Miller County Autogram-Sentinel* on September 19, 1901, reported that the mining company was erecting many fancy buildings, one of which was to have heated water, electric lights and contain a "bank, two stores, hotel, restaurant, and barber shop . . ." Additionally, a company manager was quoted as saying "Electric streetcars will be running in Enon in 14 months . . ."

But as quickly as this unprecedented growth came to the small settlement, it disappeared because of difficulties in securing financing for the mines. The mines soon closed and Enon returned to its pre-boom existence as a small, non-descript town on the Bagnell Branch of the Missouri Pacific Railroad. For decades, the foundations of the buildings erected for the erstwhile mining community were left to crumble in a pasture along a gravel road west of Enon. This road, which was once the main route through the community, has been replaced by State Highway A and the foundations have been removed.

The faith of Enon residents remained a central focus of their daily lives, inspiring a handful of those who had been attending the Rock Enon Baptist Church to establish a new congregation a few miles away in the community of Enon in 1899. The following year, the first Sunday school classes were held.

"First services were held west of the railroad tracks on the south side of McDowell Street, in a building used for a poultry and creamy buying station, which was bought by ardent Christian leader, Mrs. Mary Jane [Slayton] McGinnis," wrote Dorothy Medlen.

The church was officially organized in 1904 and was for many years known as Enon Baptist No. 2 (Rock Enon Baptist was Enon Baptist No. 1) or Enon Station. Original "Rules of Decorum" highlighted expectations of its membership and were formalized in writing shortly after the 1904 organization of the church.

"No matter of dealings against a member shall be taken unless the legal steps of the gospel according to the 18th chapter of St. Matthew have been taken except for public offenses, which may be brought first to the church," the records read.

Robert A. McGirk donated the property for a new church to be built in 1908. McGirk was the grandfather to the late Marjorie Morrow—a lifelong member of the church who played organ and piano and later finished a 43-year career as an educator after teaching at Enon School and later in Russellville.

A new church building was completed in 1909 at the cost of $1,000 and the congregation soon welcomed its first minister, Reverend James M. Henderson. There were many occasions when large baptismal events were held in the nearby Moreau River, one of which was attended by three hundred people in 1915.

The Enon Exchange Bank closed in 1931 after merging with the Russellville Exchange Bank during the Great Depression. The bank building was purchased by Enon Baptist Church in 1945 and continues to be used by the congregation for Sunday school classes and other church events. Courtesy of Jeremy P. Ämick

The next few years were defined by growth in the church and the surrounding community, highlighted by the establishment of the Enon Exchange Bank in 1916. The following year, a small brick building was erected west of the church to serve as the banking facility. John M. McGinnis, whose father helped plat Enon in 1891, was appointed to serve as the new bank's president.

The community would weather the tumultuous period of World War I and the Spanish influenza pandemic, but the advent of the Great Depression and loss of the railroad would later signal disaster for the small community and test the endurance of Enon Baptist Church.

After the completion of the Enon Exchange Bank building in 1917, the community of Enon was only a fraction of its size compared to the brief economic boom experienced in 1901 because of prospective mining operations. However, in the ensuing years, the bank and church remained key features of a community that enjoyed a strong business foundation brought on by the Bagnell Branch of the Missouri Pacific Railroad.

"Entering Enon from the east, the first building was the lumber yard operated by Bert McBroom," wrote the late Thelma Kraus in a document titled "Memories of Enon—1918." She continued, "Now you could plainly see the bright yellow depot, the agent was Herman Lessel, the railroad track and a grain elevator."

Kraus reflected upon other community businesses such as merchandise stores, a post office, and a barber shop. But while these businesses provided for the assorted personal needs of those residing in and around Enon, the church continued to serve its flock in a gospel-oriented fashion.

"[At the] revival in 1917, with Rev. J.S. Mahan, pastor, 22 were added by baptism and five by letter," wrote Dorothy Medlen in a brief church history. "In 1921, [there was] a two-week meeting with

17 additions, led by J.M. Wilcoxin, [and] at every revival many people were won to Christ."

Next door to the church, the Enon Exchange Bank began to suffer hardships following the Wall Street crash of 1929. This tumultuous period in U.S. financial history

The historic Rock Enon Baptist Church located a couple of miles northwest of Enon on State Highway V closed in 1961 after voting to merge with Enon Baptist Church. Courtesy of Christopher Jones

soon resulted in the loss of a major business anchor in the Enon community.

"A major wave of bank failures during the last few months of 1930 triggered widespread attempts to convert deposits to cash," noted an article on the FDIC website. "Confidence in the banking system began to erode, and bank runs became more common. In all, 1,350 banks suspended operations during 1930. Some simply closed their doors due to financial difficulties . . ."

An article printed in the *Jefferson City Post-Tribune* on November 20, 1931, added, "Absorption of the Enon Exchange Bank . . . by the Russellville Exchange Bank . . . was approved today by the State Finance Department."

The article continued, "The combined resources of the two banks will be over $305,000 . . . Officers of the Enon Exchange Bank, the smaller of the two, said the town was too small to support the bank."

Several years later, in 1945, the congregation of Enon Baptist Church purchased the former bank building for $300. In the coming years, as the congregation began to expand, the church was connected to the bank building to provide more space for Sunday school classes and other activities.

"Educational rooms were added to the church building and dedicated July 26, 1959," explained the 1973 booklet *Historical Sketch of Concord Baptist Association and its Churches.* It also noted during the fall of 1961, "the church bought the Frank Dawson home next door to the bank building which was remodeled and is now used as a parsonage."

For nearly six decades, Enon Baptist Church had been recognized as being spawned by Rock Enon Baptist Church located a couple of miles to the northwest on State Highway V. Sadly, on October 22, 1961, because of declining membership, the congregation of Rock Enon voted to accept an invitation to merge with Enon Baptist Church.

"Fifteen of those faithful few members attended the meeting that decided to unite with their sister church at Enon," penned Marie Rea for the 1988 Russellville sesquicentennial book. "I am sure it was a hard decision, and they regretted having to make it, but they could see no other way as the membership had become so small and expenses couldn't be met."

Then came the closure of the Bagnell Branch of the Missouri Pacific Railroad in the early 1960s, and the town's surviving business infrastructure rapidly declined. But the church, which had weather two world wars, the Great Depression, and the loss of the railroad, managed to thrive in coming years through the dedication of its congregation.

The church membership welcomed to the pulpit in 1974 Brother William B. Skelton. A combat veteran of World War II who earned a Bronze Star Medal while serving in the Philippines, Skelton conducted twenty-eight baptisms during his decade-long pastorate at Enon Baptist Church. With the small congregation unable to support a full-time pastor, Skelton taught remedial math classes at nearby Cole R-1 Elementary School during his tenure at Enon Baptist Church.

"Under the leadership of Rev. William Skelton, kitchen and restrooms were added, the bank building remodeled, also the church received a new dress all over with siding in 1978," noted a brief church history. It added, "Training Union (Baptist ministry that taught on the history and doctrine of the church) was held for years but discontinued in 1975. Sunday School was organized in 1900 and Bible School held every year since 1950 . . ."

Brother Randy Trumbo served many years as pastor at Enon, holding the distinction of being the longest-serving in the church's history. Although the original church building finished in 1908 and the former Enon Exchange Bank building continue to be used by the congregation, the parsonage was demolished many years ago and there is a parking lot where it once stood.

The businesses have faded from Enon, and the post office has been moved to Russellville. But the church, bank building and a few older homes continue to provide a reflection into the lives of those who, more than a century ago, embraced a vision for the community's continued prosperity.

"I have been a member of Enon Baptist Church since I was eight years old and I was excited that we were recently able to again remodel the old bank building," said DeeEllen Atkinson. "Over the years," she added, "our membership has changed, and we have around fifty or so members—but you always have that faithful few who are dedicated to moving everything forward. For us, the church is a major part of our lives, the history of the surrounding area, and is really the only surviving anchor left in Enon." *(Primary photograph courtesy of Jeremy P. Amick.)*

Chief Uhm Pa Tuth – *Zion Lutheran Church*

"Tell them, that the Being we all worship, under different names, will be mindful of their charity, and that the time shall not be distant, when we may assemble around his throne, without distinction of sex, or rank, or color!" wrote James Fenimore Cooper in his fictionalized novel *The Last of the Mohicans*. These words, uttered by Lieutenant General George Monro—a British military officer— might be applied to a Christian faith embraced decades later by a man who became the last Mohican chief and participated in a Lutheran ministry to Native American populations.

In the early 1940s, at a mission festival held at the former Zion Lutheran Church south of Jefferson City, Chief Uhm-Pa-Tuth regaled those in attendance with stories of faith among Native American tribes while adorned in traditional tribal clothing.

The Ravenna News (Ravenna, Nebraska) explained in its August 30, 1929, edition that he was "a full-blooded American Indian . . . who has adopted the Americanized name of Samuel Miller . . . Uhm-Pa-Tuth is the last Sachem of the Mohican tribe of Indians . . . " The newspaper continued, "The Sachem is a title given to the first Chief of the tribe and wields great influence among all the braves in his domain."

Born in 1880, Samuel Miller was raised in Shawano, Wisconsin, as a member of the Stockbridge Indians—the last remnant of the once substantial Mohican Tribe. He graduated in 1902 from Carlisle Indian Industrial School in Pennsylvania, a boarding school for Native Americans designed to help assimilate its students into American culture. In his youth, Miller also attended a small mission boarding school in the community of Red Spring operating under the umbrella of the Lutheran Church-Missouri Synod. Then, in 1913, when he was thirty-three years old, Miller was chosen to succeed his father as the new sachem, bequeathing him the title of Chief Uhm-Pa-Tuth.

"About five feet 10 inches tall, with erect carriage and keen, intelligent eyes gazing boldly from a kind and strong face, the sachem looks every inch a chief," reported the *Waterloo Evening Courier* on

July 19, 1929. The newspaper added, "To arouse interest in the [Lutheran] mission and raise funds for its enlargement, [he] has traveled over the United States to lecture before councils of his church and over the radio on the needs of the school."

Der Lutheraner, a German-language newsletter printed in St. Louis by the Lutheran Church-Missouri Synod explained the role Chief Uhm-Pa-Tuth continued to serve within the synod regarding outreach to Native Americans and fellow Lutherans. In Volume 86 of this publication printed in 1930, it noted the chief had recently spoken at an event in Albany, New York, and was described as a "fellow believer . . . whose ancestors, some centuries ago, lived almost continuously on good terms and peace with the settlers of this region."

For more than a decade, newspapers from throughout the East Coast and Midwest shared stories of Chief Uhm-Pa-Tuth's travels to

Ernest Loesch attended Chief Uhm-Pa-Tuth's lecture at Zion Lutheran Church in the late 1930s, saving this picture of the Native American leader's family.

different communities and venues to speak on the interests of Native Americans and the Lutheran church, often adorned in his full headdress.

Many of his talks, whether to large audiences gathered in an auditorium, on radio programs, or at small church picnics and mission festivals, included opportunities for him to share not only his faith but history related to his tribe.

"The Mohican/Munsee lands extended across six States from southwest Vermont, the entire Hudson River valley of New York from Lake Champlain to Manhattan, western Massachusetts up to the Connecticut River valley, Northwest Connecticut, and portions of Pennsylvania and New Jersey," explained a history listed on the website of the Mohican Nation—Stockbridge-Munsee Band.

Like many Native American tribes, the arrival of Europeans brought not only disease and war but resulted in Uhm-Pa-Tuth's ancestors being pushed out of their ancestral homelands and designation as the Stockbridge Mohicans.

The tribe eventually settled in the vicinity of Shawano County in Wisconsin and lost nearly all their reservation lands during the 1920s and 30s. Through the Indian Reorganization Act, the "Stockbridge-Munsee Community, Band of Mohican Indians" regained a large portion of their reservation accompanied by the reorganization of their tribal government.

During the more than a decade that Chief Uhm-Pa-Tuth traveled in support of the Lutheran Church-Missouri Synod, he came to Zion Lutheran Church near Jefferson City in the late 1930s, accompanied by his family.

Ernest Loesch, who grew up in the Zion community and attended Zion Lutheran Church his entire life, was in his early thirties when the chief visited the congregation and saved souvenir photographs from the event. It was a moment of connection to his great-grandfather, a founder of the church and early settler in the area, who helped carve the Zion community out of the wilderness once inhabited by Native Americans.

Years following his lecture to the Lutheran congregation at Zion, Chief Uhm-Pa-Tuth's designation as the last sachem was sealed when the Mohican Nation organized a tribal council with an elected president.

"We were told that the chief's last years were spent quietly at his Wisconsin home near Gresham, when he died at the age of 81 [in 1961]," wrote Waldemar Kautz Merrill in an article printed in the *Country Today* (Eau Claire, Wisconsin) on May 19, 2004.

The Native American leader was interred in Red Springs Cemetery in Shawano, Wisconsin.

An insightful proverb attributed to the Mohawk Tribe notes, "A good chief gives, he does not take."

Chief Uhm-Pa-Tuth embraced this sentiment, toiling for many years as a lay missionary for the Lutheran Church and speaking for equality on behalf of his fellow Native Americans living on reservations. His legacy resonates through two photographs passed down by the Loesch family and is a reminder that the last Chief of the Mohicans played an interesting and noble, albeit small, role in local religious history. *(Photographs courtesy of Candace Stockton.)*

Mt. Olive Baptist Church – *Russellville*

A group of individuals gathered in the Proctor Schoolhouse a few miles south of Russellville on June 2, 1888, taking the necessary steps to organize a Baptist church. Successful in their endeavor, it marked the beginning of Mt. Olive Baptist Church and became the second congregation founded by nearby Cole Spring Baptist Church.

Written church records note that "Cole Spring Baptist Church granted 85 brothers and sisters in Christ letters of dismission for the purpose of organizing another church of the same faith near the Pioneer Mine." After adoption of "Articles of Faith," and "Rules of Decorum," the new council and church members took a vote and chose to name their fledgling congregation "Mt. Olivet." The following year, in the fall of 1889, the church's name was changed to "Mt. Olive."

"Regular services were to be held on the first Saturday of each month and worship services on the Sunday after the first Saturday," explained the late Thelma Kraus, a member of Mt. Olive, in an article submitted for the 1988 Russellville sesquicentennial book.

An abbreviated history accessible on the church website notes, "In September 1888, the church approved construction of its first building on approximately two acres of land conveyed to the church by charter member T.J. Scott. According to recollections of stories told to long-time member Gene Steenbergen, the original building was farther west and down the hill from the present building."

Farrie L. Cole Jr. of Otterville was the longest serving pastor of Mt. Olive Baptist Church, remaining with the congregation for more than four decades.

In the early years of Mt. Olive, congregational leaders sought to ensure that church members understood their expected conduct as Christians by reading the Rules of Decorum and Articles of Faith every three months and observing the Lord's Supper on the same schedule. Congregation members failing to abide by established rules and doctrine had their behavior reviewed by an appointed committee and, if charges were found true and serious, faced possible expulsion from the church body.

An important first for the church came in 1891 when they hosted their first revival. Earliest records of Sunday school are found in church records from September 1897, when Brother Allen Scrivner was elected Superintendent of Sunday School and Joseph Amos elected the teacher.

"In April 1908, the church voted to build another new building, and construction was completed in 1909," wrote Thelma Kraus.

The new building was dedicated in May 1909 and the first church was demolished. Lumber from the old church building was used to make collection plates, one of which remains in the office of the pastor at Mt. Olive.

"My father was raised in the area and always attended Mt. Olive, so that's where I have always been a member as well," said Loretta (Scott) Raithel, who currently holds the distinction of being a member of the church for the longest period of time. "I also remember attending the first Vacation Bible School in the old building, when we used the pews for our desks. It was just a one-room building at that time with gas lights and a big stove in the front," she added.

Increasing membership and the need for additional space inspired the approval of another building program in 1949. The initiative took more than six years to yield its outcome with the dedication of a new educational annex in October 1955.

There is an impressive list of pastors who have served the congregation throughout the decades, but perhaps one of the most notable is the late Farrie L. Cole Jr., who became the longest serving pastor at Mt. Olive.

Born and raised in the community of Otterville, Cole was a graduate of Otterville High School and attended William Jewell

College. In September 1942, he was inducted into the U.S. Army and served in Central Europe as a baker and cook with the 3192nd Engineer Base Depot Company. After returning from World War II, he completed his divinity education and was ordained at his home church in Otterville in 1947. As a new pastor, Cole briefly served the congregations of Pleasant Hill Baptist Church and Corticelli Baptist Church before receiving the call to Mt. Olive on October 20, 1948.

Church history explains that Cole "has driven 30,000 miles per year visiting hospitals, nursing homes and making home visits. A car accident in 1969 left (him) recuperating for a year and drew the church members even closer together as they kept the Christian spirit going."

During Brother Cole's lengthy tenure at Mt. Olive, the church building underwent several upgrades and remodeling. In 1988, a new auditorium with a full basement was dedicated and continues to serve the congregation. In recent years, a prayer garden has been added to the church property.

The seventy-one-year-old Brother Cole retired as pastor of Mt. Olive on February 11, 1992, having dedicated more than forty-three years of his life to his church family. He passed away at the Missouri Veterans Home in Warrensburg in 2009 and was laid to rest in his hometown of Otterville.

In her many years as a member of Mt. Olive Baptist Church, Loretta Raithel has witnessed many changes. Revivals are no longer held outdoors under the protective shade of tents; the church lights are now powered by electricity instead of gas, and baptisms occur in a church baptistry, not in a local creek or stream. But through these transformations, Christian fellowship remains strong and the church body continues its history of growth.

"We have grown in a lot of ways, both spiritually and physically, and remain a mission-minded church," Raithel maintained. "And not to be too simplistic, but we are just a great group of people who

get along well and welcome all to come be part of our congregation."
(Photographs courtesy of Mt. Olive Baptist Church.)

CHAPTER 6

On the Fringe

The McKenzie House – *Henley area*

In 1829, a mere eight years after Missouri was admitted into the Union, a first-generation American born of Scottish parents purchased property in southwest Cole County. Situated on Old Forge Road a short distance from Hickory Hill, this pioneer and his family soon erected a home that continues to represent one of the few surviving examples in the area of a pre-German stone residence.

"Much of what has been written about the house claims that it was built in 1829, but that is when John Bennett McKenzie purchased the expanse of prairie land," said current owner, Jack Wills. He continued. "The house was built soon after he acquired the property and has 18-inch limestone walls built using stone that was most likely quarried about three-quarters of a mile from here in Hickory Hill."

The interior of the home was adorned with walnut trim and the construction work was predominantly done by slave labor. McKenzie lived on the property with his wife, Agnes Gibson, along with their several children. He had a row of cabins built, all of which were connected by a long porch, a short distance to the north of their home as housing for the slaves that worked on the farm.

John Bennett McKenzie was an early pioneer who settled on property near Hickory Hill in 1829 and had this home constructed, which is one of the few remaining examples of a pre-German stone residence in Cole County. The current owner, Jack Wills, has gone to great lengths to maintain the historical integrity of the house. Courtesy of Jeremy P. Amick

An undated article highlighting the home's history explained that a second, smaller home was also constructed for the farm's overseer. It notes that the house was located approximately a mile from the main McKenzie home and "is reminiscent of Tidewater [Virginia] architecture, with a huge stone chimney running through the center of the structure."

McKenzie's stone home was situated on an expanse of prairie where approaching stagecoaches could be spotted from a distance. Some historic accounts noted that he, his wife, and their family of ten children, frequently welcomed visitors traveling the nearby stage route.

Farming was not the only endeavor embraced by the early pioneer. An article printed in the *Sunday News and Tribune* on March 2, 1941, stated, "Besides operating his extensive plantation, Mr. McKenzie and his three brothers, Robert, William, and Daniel, operated a cargo train from Marion, on the river, up and down the Santa Fe Trail." The newspaper added, "He was one of the wealthiest men in central Missouri...."

In November 1867, McKenzie's wife passed away. The following summer, on July 15, 1868, he succeeded her in death. The farm and stately stone house were maintained for several years by their youngest son, James B. McKenzie, who coordinated the sale of the property in 1888.

The property entered into three generations of ownership with the Farmer family when later purchased by W.A.J. Farmer, followed by his son, Joseph Farmer. The final member of their family to own the property was James A. Farmer, who not only farmed but was employed as a yardmaster at the Missouri State Penitentiary.

In the 1950s, this small building was erected to the west of the McKenzie Home for use as a parsonage by nearby Hickory Hill Baptist Church. Courtesy of Jeremy P. Amick

"Sometime during the Great Depression, they built a barn on the west side of the house," said current property owner, Jack Wills. "I was told by one of the older residents from the area that it was a WPA [Works Progress Administration] project." He continued,

"Also, on the west side of the house is an early parsonage for the Hickory Hill Baptist Church that was built in the 1950s."

Church records indicate that another parsonage was later built closer to the church while Wills uses the former parsonage building for storage.

Following the death of James Farmer in 1955, the McKenzie Home and property were purchased by Ed Shock. Some time in past decades, the home for the overseer and the slave cabins disappeared from the property with little to denote their existence other than sparse written accounts and a hand-drawn sketch.

Wills explained, "I bought the house in 1991 and at that time, no one had lived in it since 1972. There had been remodels done around the 1940s and it had a thirty-amp electric box in the corner of one of the upper rooms and the plumbing was very primitive."

During his repairs and updates, Wills lived in the former parsonage building. Additionally, on the northeast corner of the home, there was a foundation that some records indicate was where an outdoor kitchen stood; Wills kept it and used it as the foundation for a shed. South of the house, there is a field containing more than three dozen rows of walnut trees. Wills was informed by one of the "old-timers" in the area that these trees were planted in the 1970s by Hickory Hill area resident Herbert Hahn to provide for a future walnut crop.

The McKenzie House has undergone many updates and modifications, however, Wills affirms that he has striven to find an acceptable balance between maintaining the historic integrity of the home while also creating a comfortable living space.

"The fireplaces had been covered during one of the past renovations, but I was able to expose them so that they could be used, which also reveals some of the home's original identity," he said. "Another example is the ceiling that was once in the kitchen—I uncovered that and now you can see the exposed oak timbers used as beams."

Approaching 200 years of age, the McKenzie Home has weathered the Civil War and the many ravages of time, and, like many aged citizens, has had some of its worn parts replaced. But through Wills' dedication to maintaining its historical integrity, along with the assistance of competent friends, it will be around for generations to come.

"We have sandblasted, tuckpointed, and replaced floor joists, but I have really tried to make it aesthetically accurate," said Wills. "Fortunately, I have had friends who have helped and knew what they were doing, making sure everything looks correct." He added, "It's really an interesting piece of our county history." *(Photographs courtesy of Jeremy P. Amick.)*

The Lohman Jail – *Lohman*

At a time when many local communities have demolished historic buildings with a connection to the past, the small town of

Lohman has been able to maintain much of its legacy. Not only does the town still possess the massive structure that once housed the Lohman Milling Corporation, but reveals its association with the former Bagnell Branch of the Missouri Pacific Railroad through its old depot building. Yet hidden in the shadows of the town's historic MFA Exchange sits another landmark—a small concrete jail that was erected the same year that Lohman was incorporated as a village.

"By the end of the 19th century Lohman could boast of numerous businesses, yet the town itself did not incorporate until April 7, 1910," wrote the late Gert Strobel, long-time Lohman historian, in a historical booklet printed in 1976.

During the first board meeting held several days later on April 19, 1910, George Strobel, a local stone mason who was one of the

The Lohman jail was erected by George Strobel in 1910 at a total cost of $71.00. Lohman was incorporated the same year that the jail was built and the village treasury had not yet been established, necessitating funds for the jail's construction be raised through donations from local community members and businesses.

new village's five original board members and grandfather to Gert Strobel, was elected both street commissioner and town marshal. There is no indication of a rash of crime that plagued the small village during this time, but the existence of two saloons, a pool hall, "and a couple of town characters known to enjoy their booze," served as inspiration for the erection of a jail, Gert Strobel asserted.

Having only recently been incorporated, the village of Lohman had yet to develop a revenue structure to grow its treasury. It was decided that since the jail would serve the greater good of the community by providing a place to detain anyone deemed a threat to public safety, donations were solicited from local citizens and merchants.

In 1910, the town was not only prospering from the Blochberger Saloon and other establishments serving alcohol but from the Centennial Mill, which had been moved from Millbrook four years earlier. Also, successful general stores benefitted the local economy and area farmers utilized the rail system to ship their grain and livestock to larger markets.

Gert Strobel wrote, ". . . it was reported in the meeting of August 16, 1910, that a total of $125.00 in donations had been collected. Fischer and Jungmeyer's lumber yard got a sizeable portion of that when their bill for $47.50 for supplies used in construction of the jail was approved at that time."

Recognizing his abilities as a stone mason, the board authorized Strobel to build the jail. Utilizing concrete materials, the new building, which was known locally as the "calaboose," was 12 feet wide, 14 feet long, and seven feet high. Inside, there were two small cells with a hallway in-between.

Comfort was not a consideration in the jail's construction and its rudimentary features included two mattress-free steel beds. Cost of construction soon reached $51.50 for materials and Strobel submitted a bill to the board for labor charges of $19.50. As the village grew, rules and regulations were adopted that included the licensing of saloons.

George Strobel is pictured with his wife, Anna, in the late 1930s. He served as Lohman's first town marshal and, as a stonemason, was responsible for the construction of the jail.

235

The jail weathered the changing seasons, but no records exist that might indicate it was used for anything more than a holding cell for those who imbibed a little too much. Additionally, it is believed that the small jail was last used in the 1930s.

"We purchased the property the jail sits on in the early 1980s," said Gus Fischer Jr., who was for many years a co-owner of the Lohman Milling Corporation. "The roof was in bad condition but we had it replaced a few years ago." Fischer's wife, Jeannette, added, "The gentleman who replaced the roof on the jail used to be asked by others what he was working on. He would often respond that he was repairing the Lohman Correctional Facility," she chuckled.

Gus Fischer Jr., having spent his entire life in the Lohman area, with the exception of a few years in the Navy, explained that even though there are not any sensational crime stories associated with the jail, it is a tiny building with a mammoth legacy.

"It had quit being used as a jail well before I was born but one of the interesting features is that there are marks still on the wall where somebody was counting down the time they had left before being released." He added, "There were small, one-room jails in local towns all around this area that have been demolished, but this one remains an important part of Lohman's history and is now a landmark that needs to be preserved." *(Primary photograph courtesy of Jeremy P. Ämick.)*

George Strobel, in 1911 in his capacity as town marshal, oversaw enforcement of ordinances and was even saddled with the responsibility of investigating the cost of annexing past the village's southern line.

The town marshal became the highest paying public service job in Lohman, providing a yearly salary of $50.00. Strobel held this position from April 1910 until January 1912, at which time Charles Phelen became the new marshal with J.A. Fulton serving as his deputy.

"Mr. Phelen seemed to demand all the proper instruments to go along with the job, for soon after his appointment the board spent $48.17 to purchase him a revolver, clubs, star, lock and key, cot, and blankets, purchasing items from the local firm of Soell and Kirchner," Gert Strobel shared.

The salary of the town marshal rose to $75.00 a year, however, there were added expectations such as enforcement of ordinances prohibiting livestock and other animals from running at large throughout the village. For many years, the board found it difficult to fill the role of town marshal.

Local residents have shared many stories that claim the revolver purchased for the town marshal was casually handed off to whoever was holding the position at any given time. *(Photographs courtesy of Jeremy P. Amick).*

Bicentennial Celebration – *Brazito*

The year 1976 was an exciting time for many small communities planning celebrations for the nation's bicentennial while also highlighting their own unique stories. Within the community of Brazito, one woman, who had only recently moved to the area, volunteered to chair the group that designed a bicentennial quilt featuring the area's historical buildings and spearheaded an effort to erect a monument honoring Brazito's founding families.

"My mother, Shirley Nelson, served as chairman for the Brazito Bicentennial Commission in 1976, with the help of Esther Jungmeyer as her co-chair," said Schellie Blochberger. "I believe the planning for this event began more than a year before the actual events took place," she added.

Shirley Nelson is pictured on June 19, 1976, describing the Brazito Bicentennial Quilt, which was donated to the Cole County Historical Society. Each of the thirty blocks on the quilt was embroidered with a picture of historical buildings from the Brazito area.

The kickoff occurred on March 14, 1976, when citizens of Brazito, Honey Creek and the surrounding areas gathered at the Brazito-Honey Creek Lion's Club. It was here that the bicentennial flag and certificate were presented in a ceremony attended by State Sen. Ralph Uthlaut Jr.

Receiving the certificate and flag on behalf of the community was Mrs. Marguerite Arnhold, whose late husband, Hugo, was the grandson of Christopher Arnhold—a charter member of Zion Lutheran Church near Jefferson City and the person credited with founding Brazito in 1854.

"The committee will hold its next meeting April 20 at the Brazito church to continue plans for the 'Brazito Relived' celebration, which will be held June 19," the *Daily Capital News* reported on March 11, 1976.

In preparation for the early summer bicentennial festivities, Shirley Nelson helped coordinate the collection of photographs and the creation of drawings of historic buildings in the Brazito area to be used on a Bicentennial Quilt. Stanley Carrender and Curtis Engelbrecht, both descendants of original settlers to the Brazito area, assisted Mrs. Nelson in drawing pictures of homes, barns, businesses, and other structures, many of which were no longer in existence. Oftentimes, they had only faded pictures or the memories of older residents to use when completing this task.

"They had pictures of buildings like the old Arnhold Store, the telephone building, and the gas station," recalled Schellie Blochberger. "Once these drawings were finished, my mother transferred them onto quilt blocks and a group of ladies from the community did the embroidery." She continued, "I can remember when all of the planning for this

In June 1977, a year following the bicentennial activities, this monument was dedicated outside Friedens Church to celebrate the legacy of Brazito's founders.

started, a lot of the people were a little hesitant to get involved but then it just exploded and then it seemed like they were all on board."

The local Cub Scouts also assumed an active role in preparing for the bicentennial activities by cleaning the Arnhold Cemetery. This small burial plot is where Brazito's founding father, Christopher Arnhold, was laid to rest along with many of his close relatives.

Under the guidance of adult volunteers, the Scouts also built a rustic log cabin on the property of Friedens Church. During the bicentennial celebration, the cabin was used to display antiques and crafts while also being used for historical presentations. Then came the big event on June 19, 1976. People came from far and wide for a medley of events celebrating the bicentennial featuring exhibits, patriotic music, a log sawing contest, square dance contest, cake baking contest, street dance, fashion shows, horseshoe pitching, and a mini museum inside Friedens Church.

"It was quite a day with a great turnout," said Shellie Blochberger. "There was a wooden Brazito bicentennial coin that my mother designed that was sold along with other crafts for a fundraiser."

This fundraising, along with several donations, helped fund the construction of a monument to share the story of Brazito for generations to come. On June 19, 1977, one year following the bicentennial celebration, crowds gathered in front of Friedens Church for the unveiling.

"The monument was dedicated . . . with the Immanuel Lutheran—Honey Creek church choir, invited guests and most of Brazito in attendance," explained *The Country Circuit* (monthly newsletter for Three Rivers Electric Cooperative) in its September 1977 issue. "The program included patriotic music by the church choir, the posting of colors and Pledge of Allegiance by Boy Scout Pack 16 and Girl Scouts Troop 471 Brazito-Eugene and the Invocation by the Rev. Robert Bauer, pastor of the Friedens United Church of Christ," the newsletter added.

With Shirley Nelson welcoming the guests and introducing the speakers, State Rep. Carol J. McCubbin shared a few remarks. This was followed by the monument being unveiled by Dr. William E. Parrish of Westminster College, who also served as historian for the Missouri State Bicentennial Commission. The monument remains on the grounds of Friedens Church and is dedicated to the original settlers of the Brazito area. Built from native stone, it contains a plaque sharing certain aspects of the community's history.

The legacy of Brazito's founders has been etched in history by the late Shirley Nelson, a woman with a passion for history and whose spirited leadership brought a community together for a bicentennial celebration. The Bicentennial Quilt was donated to the Cole County Historical Society for preservation and display.

"Mom passed away in 2002 and I never had the opportunity to ask what spawned her interest in preserving the history of Brazito, especially since she wasn't from the area," Schellie Blochberger explained. "She was always very involved in a number of events and organizations throughout her life, though." She added, "My mother coordinated all the promotion for the bicentennial event and worked with the powers that be to make sure it was a success. I believe that she did a remarkable job at creating her own bit of history as well." *(Photographs courtesy of Schellie Blochberger.)*

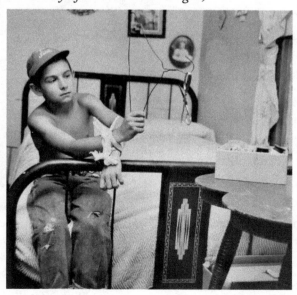

The Sommerer Hostage Situation – *Honey Creek*

An afternoon on his parents' farm near Honey Creek in late May 1960 should have been a quiet opportunity for 10-year-old George Sommerer to flip through the worn pages of his Lone Ranger comics, dreaming of the excitement of the Old West. As he then laid down for a nap, he could never have imagined waking to an event that landed his family on the pages of dozens of newspapers and a renowned national magazine.

David Parrish and Cecil Lillibridge were inmates held at the Missouri State Penitentiary in Jefferson City, both on armed robbery sentences. On May 22, 1960, they overpowered a guard and bound him, using his uniform and a prison vehicle to drive out of the front gate and onto the promise of freedom.

"They tried to stay off the major roads but made it onto Highway 54," said George Sommerer. "They turned off on our road [now Cassidy Road south of Jefferson City], not realizing it was a dead end with our house at the end of the road." Bluntly, he added, "Back then, it seemed like there was someone escaping from the penitentiary about every month or so."

Sommerer's twenty-two-year-old brother, Floyd, had been out squirrel hunting earlier in the day and returned to the house, laying his rifles down. Shortly thereafter, a knock came at the front door.

"When my brother opened the door, one of the convicts pulled a knife on him and they wrestled around a little

In late May 1960, members of the Sommerer family and Strobel family were held hostage by inmates escaped from Missouri State Penitentiary. From left: Oscar Sommerer, his mother, his son, Floyd, his wife Marie, and his youngest son, George.

bit," Sommerer said, "My grandmother started screaming and then the other convict ran from the car and popped my brother upside the head, which dazed him, and they were able to tie him up."

Quickly grabbing the rifles his brother had placed in open view, the convicts now had the upper hand. Soon, they moved the prison automobile into one of the garages on the farm since they believed they would continue their escape under the cover of darkness and didn't want to be spotted by aircraft.

"When my dad came home, they tied him up, too," Sommerer said. "My mother worked at a truck stop nearby and when she came home to help my dad do all the milking, she was also tied up."

The escapees were told that Sommerer's older sister was also working at the truck stop. When they learned that the mother was scheduled to return to work a little while later, they realized someone might come looking for her if she did not report for her shift. The escapees made the abrupt decision to depart the Sommerer Farm earlier than they initially planned.

"I had been in my room and they finally woke me up and asked if I had been playing possum," recalled Sommerer. "I told them that I

The Sommerers and Strobels were held hostage in this farm house near Honey Creek, which has since been demolished. It is pictured in this pencil drawing by Beth Bolten.

had been keeping my eyes shut but was listening to what was going on." He continued, "I can remember one of the convicts being nice and the other one being a little mean," he added. "Also, I can recall them saying that they had been treated like dogs at the penitentiary, but one only had about six months remaining on this sentence and the other about a year, I was later told."

Preparing to embark upon the next part of their escape, the convicts, after spending about three hours at the home, made sure the adults were secured, then took the ten-year-old Sommerer to one of the rooms, sitting him on the edge of the bed and binding his hands and feet with cloth strips.

They removed parts from the motors of the vehicles at the Sommerer home to prevent anyone from giving chase and then prepared to leave. It was then that a couple of unexpected guests arrived.

"Elbert and Mary Strobel lived in Jefferson City but had a farm across the street from us," Sommerer explained. "They would visit the farm on the weekends and decided to stop by our house for a visit—that's when they were seized by the convicts." Sommerer continued, "They asked Elbert [Strobel] if he had any money and he said he had just a few dollars on him. They took his wallet and found a $100

bill tucked behind some stuff and that angered one of the inmates." Pausing, he continued, "He said, 'You lied to us!' Then he put a gun to his head, and I didn't know whether he was going to shoot him."

The situation calmed and the Strobels, along with the Sommerer family, were also taken into a room and bound using cloth strips. One of the escapees was concerned that binding the hands of Sommerer's seventy-two-year-old grandmother might cut off her circulation, so they placed her on a pillow in the outhouse

A ten-year-old George Sommerer is pictured in 1960 demonstrating the ingenuity he used to free himself after being bound by two escaped prisoners from the Missouri State Penitentiary. His family's story of being held hostage appeared in Parade magazine several weeks later.

and secured the door to prevent her escape. They then stole the 1954 Chevy owned by Sommerer's brother, Floyd, since it was less likely to be noticed by law enforcement. Prior to leaving, they changed into some of the clothes of Sommerer's father and decided to take the neighbor woman, Mrs. Mary Strobel, as a hostage.

"They left sometime around 6 p.m., after being at the house for about three hours," he remarked. "In their hurry, they forgot to cut the phone line, but since we were all tied and bound, there was no way for us to call for help, anyway. But while I was sitting on the bed, tied up, I noticed a coat hanger and my mom's sewing box . . . and that gave me an idea for getting loose," he grinned.

Sommerer further explained, "Once I had the coat hanger in my tied hands, I was able to reach over to a table where my mother's sewing box was sitting and open the latch."

Once open, he was able to hook a pair of scissors with the hanger and pull them within reach of his hands. Then he managed to lift his legs and cut the binding around his feet and walk to the adjoining room, where his mother, older brother, father, and a neighbor had been similarly bound.

"I handed off the scissors to someone else, who then cut my hands loose," Sommerer said. "Then, I was able to cut everyone else loose. That's when we went and got any guns in the house that the convicts hadn't found and stolen, and then loaded them with shells in case they decided to come back."

The family went and opened the door to the out-

Francis "Bud" Jones, a Missouri State Highway Patrol officer, spotted the stolen car driven by the escapees while on patrol near Olean. Courtesy of Jeremy P. Ämick

house, where the convicts had earlier locked up Sommerer's seventy-two-year-old grandmother. Finally, they telephoned the Missouri State Highway Patrol and within about fifteen minutes, the first troopers arrived. They explained to the troopers the details of their brief captivity, the theft of the 1954 Chevy, and that their neighbor, Mrs. Mary Strobel, had been taken hostage.

Earlier, the convicts shared with the Sommerer family that they were making their getaway to the Kansas City area, asking what roads they should travel in order to elude the authorities. The family offered suggestions and were therefore able to describe to the troopers the most likely route they would be driving. The call went out on the police radios and the search began for the 1954 Chevy that had been stolen from Sommerer's older brother, Floyd.

"Before being spotted by the patrolman, the car had wound over the back roads in the vicinity of Russellville and other communities in Cole, Moniteau, and Miller Counties," reported the May 31, 1960, edition of the *St. Louis Globe Democrat*. The newspaper added, "Sgt. F.A. Jones, patrolling a country road near Olean . . . spotted a car which looked like the one stolen by the escapees. He approached close enough to check the license number and radioed for verification of the identity."

One of the escapees fired the stolen .22 rifle at the state trooper and the bullet went through the windshield and struck the patrolman on his Sam Brown belt. Fortuitously, the small caliber of the bullet along with the window slowing the bullet's speed and the thick leather halted the projectile to the extent that it fell to the floor of the car without any serious injury to the patrolman.

"It was lucky that we didn't have any higher caliber rifles in the house for the convicts to steal because that probably would have meant the death of Sgt. Jones," Sommerer glumly noted.

Sgt. Jones backed off a short distance in his pursuit. The escapees soon lost control of the 1954 Chevy, careening into a ditch and coming to rest against a tree. The two men bolted into the woods to continue their escape, leaving the uninjured Mrs. Strobel in the automobile.

"In later years, Mary Strobel told me that the scariest part of the ordeal was having to cross the field to Sgt. Jones because there was a bull in the field," Sommerer said. "But she was able to make it across without incident."

Next came the Highway Patrol's helicopter and bloodhounds to assist with the backwoods search. Around 11 p.m. in the evening, the excitement of the day came to an end when the escapees surrendered to authorities after seeking concealment in a cemetery near Olean.

All but one of the major characters in the kidnapping—the two escaped convicts, Sommerer's grandmother, father, older brother, mother, and their neighbors—have since passed away. But as Sommerer excitedly explained, it became a widespread event that brought his family a few moments of unexpected fame.

"My father had a farm truck with his name painted on the side of it and when we would drive into town, people would point at it because they recognized our name and associated it with the event," he said. "That was quite an experience for me, being I was only ten years old when it all happened."

Sommerer continued, "Not too long after this happened, we were contacted by Parade magazine and they offered to pay us to share the story. We ended up receiving $100 for the story and split it five ways between me, my father, mother, older brother, and grandmother," he added, holding up a time-worn copy of Parade dated August 7, 1960. He concluded, "The year before, there had been a farm family taken hostage and murdered in Kansas. We may have become the talk of the town locally, but we were very fortunate and appreciative of the quick response of law enforcement in the area." *(Photographs courtesy of George Sommerer.)*

Memories of a Tugboat Dock and Prison Saw Mill *– Henley area*

When Gene Snellen drives along South Teal Bottom Road near Henley, approaching his home along the Osage River, he is often reminded of points of historical interest and moments spent with his grandfather. It is a journey through time that helps preserve the legacy of a tugboat operation that existed along the river and a nearby prison sawmill established during the 1960s.

"My grandfather, Myron Snellen, lived in Jefferson City but he would come out to our farm, which at the time was on property owned by Orlando Hickey," said Gene Snellen. "There were six rental cabins on the property that had in earlier years been used by railroad workers," he continued. "Orlando Hickey eventually turned them into rental cabins and my grandfather would come down here and rent one of the cabins so that he could fish the Osage."

Gene Snellen was about five years old when he began accompanying his grandfather on his trips to the cabin. He was told about an old tugboat operation that had used a nearby dock, but by then, all that remained of it were a few pylons protruding from the murky waters of the Osage River.

In an article appearing in the *Miller County Autogram*-Sentinel on December 16, 1926, it was reported, "In 1898, the Anchor Milling

The "RUTH" Owned by Anchor Milling Co.
THE ROCK ISLAND RAILROAD BRIDGE NEAR HOECKER, MISSOURI

Company, desiring to expand its business, began the construction of a boat at Tuscumbia to be 110 feet long and with a 20-foot beam,"

The article further noted of the Tuscumbia-

Years ago, Snellen was given this photograph of the "Ruth," a tugboat from Tuscumbia that used the dock located on his property just south of the railroad bridge.

based company, "Local crews were employed on this boat, and during the boating season it was almost continuously engaged in hauling out wheat, barytes, lumber, livestock, kaolin, and other products as well as bringing up merchandise from Osage City and Hoecker."

Hoecker was a small community located east of Henley in Miller County. Springing up on the farm of Joseph Hoecker. The settlement came into existence with the construction of the Rock Island Railroad; however, just like the railroad, it has since disappeared. As Snellen learned from his grandfather and others from the area, the tugboats used the dock for years to load and deliver many types of general freight. But when the Rock Island Railroad came through the area in the early 1900s, it brought an end to this business endeavor.

Snellen explained that his family moved to Mexico when he was a young boy and that he lived in Rolla for many years. When he was fifteen years old, his family returned to Jefferson City, where he graduated from Jefferson City Senior High School in 1973. Throughout his childhood, he enjoyed spending countless summers and weekends with his grandfather at his cabin, both fishing and exploring the area. During these trips, he witnessed another interesting activity in the area that has nearly been forgotten.

"When you turn onto South Teal Bottom Road from Highway H, before you enter into Henley, there are two buildings on opposite sides of the roads that were once barracks used by prisoners from the penitentiary," Snellen said. "Basically, they were trustees that ran a prison sawmill," he added.

"Gov. James T. Blair Jr., Friday signed leases for a sawmill farm to be operated by the Department of Corrections near Henley . . ." the *Miller County Autogram-Sentinel* reported on March 24, 1960. "The 700 acres are on the Orlando Hickey farm, across the road from the Spring Valley brick school building."

The school building referenced in the aforementioned newspaper article still stands and is now used as a house of worship by the Spring Valley Baptist Church.

"There was a sawmill built by a small pond and I remember going there with my grandpa in his truck to get a load of firewood for the cabin," said Snellen. "The prisoners would stack the wood in the bed of the truck and we would be charged fifty cents for the entire load." He added, "They also sawed logs and then made fenceposts that they creosoted. There were quite a few prisoners living there—at least enough for a couple softball teams because I recall seeing them play when we drove by."

The *Daily Capital News* reported on January 12, 1966, "The third unit of Prison Farms is tucked away in the hills near Henley. Here timber is cut from 700 acres of leased land and processed by an open saw under a tin-roofed building."

The article also described the farm as a light security unit with approximately forty-five to fifty inmates living and working there.

This lack of direct oversight by prison guards inspired a unique tale passed down to Snellen.

"Years ago," Snellen recalled, "Lloyd Belt told me that he used to ride his horse to the old bar in Henley and there would be a different prisoner in t every night wearing the same set of civilian clothes." Chuckling, he added, "I guess the prisoners had only one set of non-work clothes and would pass them among each other, and then one wearing them would walk the mile or so to Henley in the evening to have a couple of beers."

The prison farm closed down in the late 1960s. Several years later, in 1979, Snellen purchased a large tract of property that once belonged to Orlando Hickey, upon which sits the old cabin where he and his grandfather shared many memorable moments.

"My grandfather passed away when he was seventy-three years old and the railroad closed in 1979," Snellen said. "The piers from the old tugboat dock are now gone and the cabin he rented for so long is no longer habitable. But when I came here as a child, this was like traveling to the middle of nowhere and was as exciting as going to Disneyland . . . well, at least for me. One thing is for certain, this area has seen a lot of history and I am glad that I had the opportunity to witness some of it." *(Photographs courtesy of Gene Snellen.)*

Morris Burger – *Red Brush Community*

Born in 1935 and raised on a farm with no electricity, running water, or an indoor restroom, Morris Burger learned at an early age how to function under meager circumstances. Years later, as he prepared to assume a leadership role in Burgers' Smokehouse, the business established by his father, his childhood experiences and service with the U.S. Army during the Cold War provided him with the managerial and interpersonal skills to be successful.

Burger recalled, "We lived in the rural Red Brush Community nine miles southwest of California, and that's where I grew up with my older sister Mary and younger sister Jane." He added, "Some people would call us poor and perhaps we were, but we didn't know it because we didn't have rich neighbors to compare ourselves to."

Like so many who came of age in rural Moniteau County communities during and following the Great Depression, a young Morris

Burger was imbued with an unyielding work ethic while working on both his father's farm and that of his grandparents, Fred and Minnie Bueker.

The first seven years of his education were received at Red Brush School—a one-room schoolhouse where a single teacher instructed children of varying ages. He later transferred to California High School, where he played basketball and ran track. Additionally, he was active in the Future Farmers of America, serving as his chapter's president and earning the designation of "State

Morris Burger grew up on a small farm southwest of California. After attending a one-room schoolhouse, he transferred to California High School. When graduating in 1953, he enrolled at the University of Missouri and received his first military experience in the school's ROTC program.

Farmer" in 1953. In 1952, a one-room building known as the "Ham House" was erected on his Grandfather Bueker's farm to be used by Burger's father for the curing of hams. This operation in the coming years evolved into the business known as Burgers' Smokehouse.

"The champion light ham, exhibited by Morris Burger of California, was purchased at $7 a pound . . .," noted the *Kansas City Times* on August 25, 1953, when reporting on happenings at the Missouri State Fair.

Burger explained, "Upon graduation in 1953, I intended to work on the farms. However, my Aunt Lena Bueker Bieri thought I should go to college. Enrolling at the University of Missouri turned out to be a very smart move."

Admitting that he did not earn an "impressive" record of academic achievement in high school, Burger was dedicated to his collegiate studies and achieved top academic awards. While in college, he joined all able-bodied males in completing two years of mandatory participation in the Reserve Officer Training Corps (ROTC).

"The military seemed to be a good fit for me," wrote Burger. "The curriculum, the discipline, and the encouragement from Colonel Frank Skelly, who was in charge of the Army ROTC program at MU, contributed to my military experience."

Embracing the regimented structure of the ROTC, Burger remained in the program during his final two years of college. In the summer of 1956, between his junior and senior years, he received a taste of the active military experience by attending a summer camp at Fort Sill, Oklahoma, finishing fourth out of 96 cadets in the training.

Graduating in late spring of 1957 with a degree in Agriculture Engineering, Burger was also commissioned a second lieutenant in the United States Army. In later years, he beamed with pride when sharing the memory of this mother pinning the new officer's rank on his uniform. Lt. Burger had a two-year active-duty commitment to fulfill and embarked upon his new military journey by completing seventeen weeks of initial officer's training at Fort Sill. Assigned to Field Artillery, he learned to "fire a wide variety of weapons safely, hand to hand combat training and chemical warfare, (and) . . . a lot of classroom training related to Field Artillery."

He further explained, "For artillery weapons to be successful, you have to be knowledgeable in fire direction and survey. Both of these areas require advanced mathematics. My [college] degree along with a Military Occupational Specialty made this fairly easy for me."

When successfully completing the training in late 1957, the young lieutenant was offered the opportunity to remain at Fort Sill and instruct subsequent classes. However, being young and seeking adventure, he declined and instead received orders assigning him to a unit in Germany. Upon reporting to his

Morris Burger was commissioned a second lieutenant in the U.S. Army following his graduation from college in 1957. He later served with a field artillery battery in Germany during the Cold War. After his discharge, he served with an Army Reserve unit in Tipton and went to work for his father's business, Burgers' Smokehouse.

new duty assignment with a field artillery battalion in Baumholder, Germany, Lt. Burger met Bill Tweedie, the soldier he was replacing. The two visited and Burger learned that Tweedie was from Jefferson City and a member of the family that owned Tweedie Shoe Factory. Established in 1884 by local merchant John Scrivner, the community of Scrivner is now little more than a scattered

Morris recalled, "Many of the older senior officers at the battalion level were married while many of the younger lieutenants in line batteries were, like me, single. We were in our early twenties. It was our first time away from home and they seemed to take pity on or felt sorry for us."

As the commander of a field artillery battery within the division, Burger was given a top security clearance to attend the 7th Army Weapons Assembly School. It was there that he learned the processes for assembling and handling nuclear-armed munitions.

"There was a lot of travel related to military assignments," Burger recalled of his time overseas. "We went on a number of different maneuvers with the entire unit to other areas. For example, we had a Rhine River crossing at Karlsruhe where the engineers created bridges for us to cross major streams." Recognizing the importance of this training within an area of Europe where there were obvious tensions between the Soviet Union and the U.S., he added, "This practice was necessary because in wartime, bridges and rails are the first to be blown up."

In September 1960, the year following his release from active duty, Morris Burger married Dolores Harlan at First Baptist Church in California.

As a farm kid who had seen little of the world outside of Moniteau County prior to joining the U.S. Army, Morris Burger found himself on the front lines of the Cold War in Germany in 1958. Though just an untested young officer in command of a field artillery battery possessing nuclear capabilities, he and his fellow soldiers continued to train in the event a conflict erupted between the U.S. and the Soviet Union.

"We . . . took our entire battalion to our annual Seventh Army tests that took place east of Nuremberg at a base called Grafenwoehr," Burger wrote in his later years. "Our mission was to give atomic support to the British ground [forces], gaining arms such as their infantry and armor." He added, "At the time, Germany was divided among the Allies. The British occupied the northern part, the French a smaller section in the middle and the U.S. the larger central and southern region."

During training exercises near the Czechoslovakian border, Burger recalled that staff from the Seventh Army evaluated the readiness and performance of each of their battalion's gun sections. In the end, his section was recognized as the best M65 atomic gun crew in the entire Seventh Army in Germany. To celebrate their achievements, the soldiers walked to the nearby border of Czechoslovakia—a Warsaw Pact country that was at the time under the control of the Soviet Union—and engaged in an act that had been popularized in World War II.

"The celebration ended when we went to the fence at the border and urinated through the Iron Curtain into Czechoslovakia," he mirthfully recalled. "Lucky for us, it was not an electric fence."

During the United States' crossing of the Rhine River in March 1945, General Patton urinated into the river from a pontoon bridge, symbolizing United States' historic entrance into Germany.

In his position as a junior officer, Lt. Burger was frequently required to serve an overnight shift as the battalion duty officer. During New Year's Eve 1958, while fulfilling such a duty, he was contacted by a sergeant requesting that he come to their barracks immediately. When arriving at the scene, he observed a highly intoxicated and belligerent enlisted soldier sporting for a fight with anyone who might oblige him. Burger confronted the soldier and was met with the blunt reply, "I'm going to kill every (expletive) lieutenant in the United States Army!"

He said, "A brief conversation followed. When he started to come toward me, I pulled out a loaded 45-caliber pistol and chambered a bullet. I told him if he took one more step, he would be heading for the hospital." Continuing, he added, "The bullet being chambered broke the eerie silence and had an immediate sobering effect on him. He stopped and hung his head in a quiet surrender."

Burger then instructed some of the enlisted men who witnessed the event to put the intoxicated soldier in bed and for the sergeant to have him report to his office the following afternoon, on New Year's Day.

"When he met with me, he was the most respectful, contrite young man I have ever seen," he wrote. "I told him I was not going to report the incident or charge him with anything . . . since he did obey my order. He went away sobbing, apologizing, and thanking me for not causing more trouble for him."

Two weeks following this incident, Burger was promoted to first lieutenant. The next several months of his overseas assignment fell into something of a routine as he gained experience and confidence as an officer. Several months later, in June 1959, having completed his active-duty commitment, he boarded an airplane and returned to the states.

Shortly after receiving his discharge, Burger joined his father's expanding business, Burgers' Smokehouse. He also made the decision to propose to his fiancée, Dolores, and the couple married on September 10, 1960, at First Baptist Church. In the coming years, they raised two sons and a daughter.

"My Army career in the active reserves continued for another five years," Burger explained. "It consisted of training one night each week and one two-week summer camp each year. The weekly training occurred at Tipton." He further noted, "The unit at Tipton was small, maybe 18 to 22 soldiers. I was the commanding officer for the last three years. It was easy duty . . . (w)e were a live and let live bunch."

While finishing out his military career with the Tipton unit, he was promoted to the rank of captain.

Morris Burger was an active member and supporter of many benevolent organizations and received several accolades throughout the years. Yet one of his most enduring legacies has been his association with Burgers' Smokehouse and helping to grow the company into a nationally recognized brand prior to his retirement in 2000. Following a lengthy and resurgent battle with cancer, the eighty-five-year-old veteran passed away on December 16, 2020. His military experiences, Burger often explained, provided a leadership foundation that inspired success in many facets of his daily life.

"After he finished his overseas service, my father came home and got involved with the family business and rarely spoke about his military service," said Steven Burger. "But he was proud of being the first of his family to attend college and likewise, being able to fulfill his ambition of becoming an officer in the Army."

He concluded, "The military opened up the world for him and he credited those experiences as a large part of the leadership development that helped him successfully guide the business in later years." *(Photographs courtesy of Steven Burger.)*

Bibliography

Abilene Reporter-News. "Historic St. Joseph a Big Part of Town's Celebration." September 2, 1995.

Berwyn Life. "Mechanics Give 'On-the-Line' Aid." March 21, 1945.

California Democrat. "Rev. Jos. Residorf ..." November 23, 1876.

Central Missouri Leader. "New Blacksmith Shop." December 9, 1921.

Cole County Weekly Rustler. "Hemstreet Bridge." April 8, 1927.

Collier, Doris Scrivner. *The Descendants of Benjamin Scrivner*. D.S. Collier: MO, 1990.

Country Today. "Meeting the state's last Mohican Chief." May 19, 2004.

Daily Capital News. "Bicentennial Ceremony Set." March 11, 1976.

———. "First Class Rating to Harmony Grove School." December 25, 1946.

———. "Former Slave Dies at Centertown at Age of 113 Years." *March 2, 1945.*

———. "Endicott Case is Up: All Russellville Here." November 17, 1920.

———. "Huff Wins Case in Circuit Court." March 9, 1943.

———. "News of Cole County." January 5, 1923.

———. "Prison Industries, Farms Grow." January 12, 1966.

———. "School Days." June 5, 1976.

Eldon Advertiser. "County Correspondence." September 29, 1910.

———. "Death of J.M.T. Miller." June 6. 1918.

———. "Eugene Receives $600,000 From Bonds." July 12, 1984.

———. "Mary Gertrude Taylor." February 14, 1985.

———. "Miller County Founded 150 Years Ago This Month." February 19. 1987.

———. "Minister's and Deacon's Meeting." October 27. 1904.

———. "Olean." December 31, 1914.

———. "Russellville Teacher Killed, Three Injured in Accident." November 30, 1989.

———. "The Way It Was." September 15, 1988.

English, Jr., George H. *History of the 89th Division, U.S.A.* Denver, CO: Smith-Brooks Printing Co., 1920.

Federal Deposit Insurance Corporation. "Managing the Crisis: The FDC and RTC Experience—Chronological Overview." Accessed February 28, 2023. https://www.fdic.gov/bank/historical/managing/chronological.

Ford, James E. *A History of Jefferson City, Missouri's State Capital, and of Cole County.* Jefferson City, MO: New Day Press, 1938.

Gaul, Jeffrey. *History of the Third Infantry Division: Rock of the Marne.* Nashville, TN: Turner Publishing Company, 1988.

Hiller, Walter. *History of the 1264th Engineer Combat Battalion.* Goppingen, Germany: Druckerei Kirchner, September 1945.

History of Cole, Moniteau, Morgan, Benton, Miller, Maries and Osage Counties, Missouri. Chicago, IL: Goodspeed Publishing Company, 1889.

Illustrated Daily News. "Man Exonerated in Woman's Death." December 30, 1933.

Illustrated Sketchbook & Directory of Jefferson City and Cole County, Missouri, 1900. Capital City Family Research, 1900.

Jefferson City Republican. "Here and There." March 31, 1904.

Jefferson City Post-Tribune. "Dixie Gardens Will Open Wednesday." November 22, 1930.

———. "Enon Exchange Bank Goes to Russellville." November 20, 1931.

———. "Judge Smith Dies at Home Near Henley." March 30, 1933.

———. "News of the Community." April 20, 1929.

———. "News of the Community: Centertown." September 24, 1931.

———. "Pleasant Hill." July 1, 1929.

———. "Pleasant Hill." January 3, 1930.

———. "R-IV to Send Students to City." July 10, 1953.

Kansas City Star. "District to Build One-Room Schoolhouse as Tribute." June 11, 1998.

Kansas City Times. "A Welcome by Donnelly." August 25, 1953.

Koester, Reba A. *The Heritage of Russellville in Cole County.* Jefferson City, MO: self-published, 1977.

Lincoln Clarion. "Oldest Voter." December 1, 1944.

Los Angeles Times. "A Fight with Bandits." February 28, 1895.

Miller County Autogram-Sentinel. "A Story of Steamboat Days on the Osage River, and the Part River Navigation Took in the Development of Miller County." December 16, 1926.

———. "Etterville." September 22, 1910

———. "Eugene No. 2." May 21, 1942.

———. "Henley, Mrs. Otto Bruce." August 19, 1937.

———. "Prison Sawmill Farm Begins Operation on Leased 700-acre Site Near Henley." March 24, 1960.

———. "Those Mines at Enon." September 19, 1901.

Missouri State University. "One Room Schoolhouse: Celebrating a Legacy." Accessed March 3. 2023. https://education.missouri-state.edu/OneRoomSchoolhouse.htm.

Moniteau County, Missouri Family History Book: A History of Moniteau County and Its People. California, MO: Moniteau County Historical Society, 1980.

National Archives and Records Administration. "World War I Draft Registration Cards." Accessed March 2, 2023. https://www.archives.gov/research/military/ww1/draft-registration.

National Park Service. "One Room Schools in the Ozarks." Accessed March 4, 2023. https://www.nps.gov/ozar/learn/historyculture/one-room-schools-in-the-ozarks.htm.

Pleasant Hill Times. "Second to None." March 20, 1914.

Ohio Public Health Journal. "Light." Volume VII, 1917, p. 63.

Osage Valley Banner. "Cole Spring Picnic." August 14, 1879.

Raithel, Erna. *Russellville, Missouri, Sesquicentennial: 1838-1988.* Versailles, MO: B-W Graphics, Inc. 1988.

Ravenna News. "Chief Uhm-Pa-Tuth to Give Sunday Lecture." August 30, 1929.

Sedalia Democrat. "A Splendid Resort." April 3, 1900.

——. "Fire Destroys Dixie Gardens." August 6, 1947.

——. "New Companies Incorporated." July 27, 1900.

——. "Wholesale Liquors." October 4, 1908.

St. Louis Globe-Democrat. "Boy's Resourcefulness and Effective Dragnet Help Capture Convicts." May 31, 1960.

Scheperle, Palmer. *History of the Scheperle (Schepperle) Family of America.* Jefferson City, MO: Modern-Litho Print, 1982.

State Republican. "Zion Items." January 28, 1892.

Sunday News and Tribune. "Library Activity Pictured." October 15, 1950.

——. "Local Hunters Leave for Colorado Friday." October 16, 1960.

——. "New Roads Ease Holiday Trip." April 27, 1969.

——. "$103,035 Went to Cole County CWA Workers." April 1, 1934.

——. "School Auction." March 16, 1958.

——. "You Can Still Find Engelbrecht Name in Ambrose Club." October 4, 1970.

Tipton Times. "Announcement." October 22, 1937.

——. "Cities on Highways." December 25, 1925.

——. "Club Notes." May 17, 2001.

——. "Putnam-Gabert Chevrolet Company." September 5, 1958.

Waterloo Evening Courier. "Last Mohicans Live in Wisconsin." July 19, 1929.

Warman-Stallings, Kelly. *The Ghost Towns of Central Missouri, Volume 1.* Jefferson City, MO: Ketch's Printing, 1993.

Westliche Post. "Aus Missouri und den Nachbarstaaten." August 6, 1910.

Word and Way. "Hickory Hill Church, Concord Association." November 7, 1935.

Index

Printed in the USA
CPSIA information can be obtained
at www.ICGtesting.com
LVHW041056171223
766701LV00043B/467

9 781957 262901